PAKISTAN
AND
UNTOUCHABILITY

CH. AFZAL HAQ
(AHRAR)

MAKTABA-E-URDU
LAHORE

The original published cover of Pakistan and Untouchability, by
Chaudhry Afzal Haq, 1941

Pakistan
and
Untouchability

A banned book that was no longer in circulation

Chaudhry Afzal Haq

2014 International Edition

www.ChaudhryAfzalHaq.com
www.PakistanAndUntouchability.com

Pakistan and Untouchability
May 1941
(Ahrar)
Originally Published by Ch. Nazir Ahmed, Proprietor Maktaba-e-Urdu
15 Circular Road, Printed at the New Union Press, 53 Circular Road, Lahore.
2014 Edition Published by Createspace

ISBN: 1494937034

ISBN 13: 9781494937034

A young British Punjab Police Sub-Inspector, Chaudhry Afzal Haq

The Story of The Original Published Book, Pakistan And Untouchability

The original hard copy book was one of the last copies of *Pakistan and Untouchability* known to us at the time. This original printed book was a banned book that was rescued from being destroyed in Pakistan by Jim Hurley, who was Vice Consul at the U.S. Consulate in Lahore, West Pakistan, in 1955-60. He concealed this book and took it out of West Pakistan to Burma for safekeeping until he eventually opened a rare books dealership on the east coast of the United States. This original hardback book had been a little known and banned book since then. This copy of the original book cover was taken from this same book now located in Switzerland at our cousin's home.

I came to read the original hard copy of *Pakistan and Untouchability* at my cousins' house in Switzerland in 1996 for the first time. My German born cousin, Dr. Homayon had searched for a copy of this book for years. Just a few months prior to my visit with him, and just by chance, he located the original book from the same Jim Hurley who was now a rare books dealer.

About The Photo Of Chaudhry Afzal Haq On The Cover Of This Book

The photograph on the cover of this book was taken after his release from Rawalpindi Jail and a year before his death in 1942. He was only 48 years old.

Acknowledgements

We thank Mr. Jim Hurley, American Consul in Lahore, West Pakistan in 1955, for rescuing an original copy of this book from Governmental confiscation. I am also very grateful to my cousin Dr. Homayon in Switzerland, grandson of Chaudhry Afzal Haq, for locating and obtaining that same original copy from Mr. Hurley and providing it to me as the manuscript for this new 2014 International version of Pakistan and Untouchability. Without my cousins lifelong and shared interest in our grandfather's life, this project would not have been possible.

My big thank you also goes to the many people who provided information and guidance to the project, including our uncle Colonel (Ret) Izhar-ul-Haq-Adeeb (son of the late author), Ch. Ihsan-ul-Haq (nephew of the late author), and Rana Aurangzeb (friend to the family).

A warm appreciation also goes to Syed Kafeel Shah Bukhari, the grandson of Syed Ataullah Shah Bukhari, for his guidance. Syed Ataullah Shah Bukhari was a most respected spiritual leader and founding member of Majlis-e-Ahrar-e-Islam. Syed Ataullah Shah Bukhari was a very close friend and colleague of Chaudhry Afzal Haq during his lifetime and deserves much credit for inspiring Afzal Haq to embark on a lifetime of public service and resistance to foreign occupation.

Contents

Contents (continued)

Introduction In 2014

The creation and freedom of Pakistan, and today's India, from Colonial British rule had not occurred at the time of the original publication of this book in 1941. Chaudhry Afzal Haq lays out convincing and reasoned arguments as to why the creation of Pakistan will be unavoidable unless there is a fundamental change in the hearts and minds of the Indian people. In this book, he examines the conditions that would later make the division of the subcontinent, and creation of Pakistan, inevitable.

"I come to the reasonable conclusion that the Hindu-Muslim problem is not a religious one, and that we must find out those causes that are responsible for the present state of affairs in the country." - Chaudhry Afzal Haq, *Pakistan and Untouchability*

Born before the turn of the 20th century, Chaudhry Afzal Haq was commissioned as a young police officer, in 1917. During the next few years, he was witness to many incidents of unbridled atrocities by the British rulers, such as the unprovoked massacre in Jallianwalla Bagh in Amritsar.

Disillusionment with, and rebellion against foreign domination must have gradually developed to a crescendo in his consciousness. Eventually, in 1922, while on intelligence duty of a public gathering of the nationalist movement, he was profoundly inspired and moved by Syed Ataullah Shah Bukhari's impassioned speech against British rule. Sub-Inspector Chaudhry Afzal Haq resigned his police post, right then and there, and joined the nationalist movement. This event was seen as a treasonous act against British rule. As punishment, and deterrent to others, he was immediately arrested and brutally tortured.

Subsequently, he began public speaking, writing, and political activities against the colonial occupation of the Subcontinent. As a result, he was sent to prison quite frequently during his two- decade long peaceful leadership of the nationalist resistance movement against British domination.

In time, he was recognized as a formidable political leader of his time, who was respected by his supporters as well as his opponents. As an elected member of the Punjab's Provincial Legislative Assembly, his special focus was on human rights related issues, new jail reform laws, agriculture regulations, education, as well as many other public welfare efforts.

History will also remember him as an important writer of his time. During his political career, he would go on to write a total of 16 books on political, religious and social topics. His writings reflect his intense desire to promote social and economic justice for the common people through societal change using educational and political processes. Afzal Haq had a life-long passion for writing and often wrote from the harsh settings in each prison where he was confined. Most of his books were written in Urdu and are available in the bookstores of Pakistan.

Pakistan and Untouchability was written in English by Chaudhry Afzal Haq and published in 1941. This book was banned from publication by the Pakistan Government, after 1947, out of some unknown political fear. Hence, it has been out of publication and unavailable to readers for the past many years. We have decided to make it available for interested readers because of its historical perspective. Historically, the book presents a clear analytical picture of the cultural-political causes that led to the 1947 partition and the tragic events that followed it. Aside from its historical importance, the book is enlighteningly relevant in understanding the current, dangerous, turmoil in the same geopolitical region.

Mrs. Najum S. Khan
(Daughter of Ch. Afzal Haq)
May 15, 2014

Quotes from those who knew Ch. Afzal Haq

"Our nation has totally forgotten a great and respectable personality like Chaudhry Afzal Haq."

Abu Yousaf Qasmi, Writer, *Chaudhry Afzal Haq (Qasmi.prologue.)**

"Chaudhry Afzal Haq was a great human being. We left the duty of "thinking" to him, but it does not mean that he was not a man of practical politics. Though naturally he was a careful man, but whenever the party decided to fight a political battle, he also fought like a true soldier." "He was such a great person that he didn't even like to insult his opponents."

Syed Ataullah Shah Bukhari *(September 23, 1892 - August 21, 1961) was a Muslim Scholar, Religious and Political leader and one of Majlis-e-Ahrar-e-Islam's founding members. His greatest contribution had been his germination of strong anti-British feelings among the Indian Muslims. (Qasmi.chapter2*)*

"During our discussion meetings, I realized that his mental acuity and his understanding of issues was quite superior. I was often surprised at the balanced, in-depth and mature analysis of the current political scene which he presented...In the Punjab Legislative assembly, his speeches were always so fact-based, and powerfully persuasive that even the Government benches admitted of his greatness."

Maulana Ghulam Rasul Mehr, Writer and Scholar (1893 - 1971) *(Qasmi, p. 60)**

"Ch. Afzal Haq organized the Arhar party in such a way that other major parties of India paled in comparison...He was a guiding light for us all."

Sheikh Hissam-ud-Din *(June 1, 1897- June 21-1967) was an important figure in the politics of Punjab and a leader of All India Majlis-e-Ahrar-ul-Islam. He was of Secretary General of Majlis-e-Ahrar-e-Islam Pakistan in 1958. (Qasmi, p. 35, 38)**

"Through his habit of altruism and self-sacrifice, he always preferred the common good to any personal comfort. He felt such contentment and joy in working for the welfare of common people that you will not find in other Muslim leaders of today."

Khawaja Abdul-Rehman Ghazi (Qasmi.p.74)*

*All quotes above and on the back of the book cover are from Abu Yusuf Qasmi, *Ch. Afzal Haq,* *bisat-e-Adab Publishers, Lahore, Pakistan, 1991.*

The literary works of Chaudhry Afzal Haq

To fully appreciate the life and works of Chaudhry Afzal Haq, read his many other books, including the award winning *Zindagi* (Life) and his autobiography *Mera Afsana* (My Life). Both are currently in process of being republished in English and the new Documentary Film, Chaudhry Afzal Haq, An Untold Story is due for release in 2015. His other major books available in Urdu are Deene Islam, Mahboobe Khuda , Jawahrat, Shaoor, Dehati Rooman, Tareekhe Ahrar Khatoote Afzal Haq

Information on all this is available on:

www.ChaudhryAfzalHaq.com
www.PakistanAndUntouchability.com

National flag of the United Kingdom flying over British India in 1941

Source: Courtesy of Wikipedia

Flag of Imperial India in 1941
Chaudhry Afzal Haq and all Indians also watched this flag flying
over their India in 1941

Source: Courtesy of Wikipedia

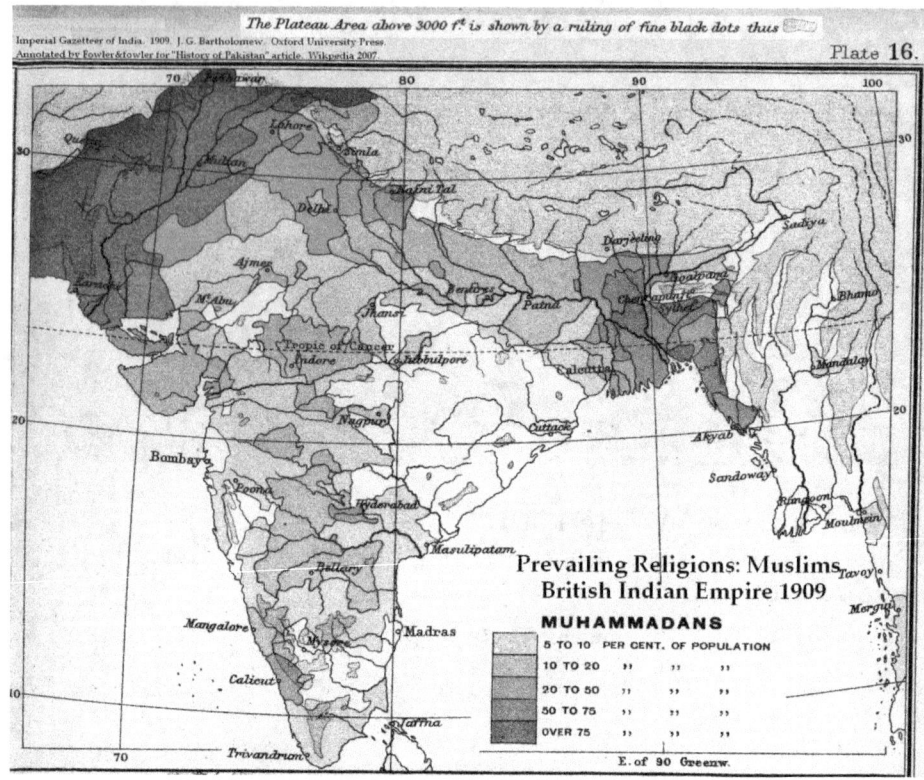

Muslim Percentage in India during the time Chaudhry Afzal Haq was a young man just after the turn of the 20th century.

Source: Courtesy of Wikipedia

Foreword

The communal question has grown so serious in India, especially since the inauguration of the Provincial Autonomy, that [the dream of a nation called] Pakistan has been prescribed to be the only panacea for all the Muslim ills. The Muslim League sees no other way of consolidating the position of the Musalmans of India, except by establishing a separate homeland for themselves. But if this scheme, which aims at the segregation of Indian Muslims, is examined critically and rather dispassionately, the sane-minded Muslims shall undoubtedly arrive at the conclusion that it is not a religious movement at all, but a movement solely inspired and engineered by political leaders who simply exploit the religious susceptibilities of the Muslim masses. It is the primary need of the occasion that this vital issue must be analyzed and judged at its intrinsic value. Although much has been said for and against the proposed scheme, I find that there is scope still for a disinterested commentary. The following few pages are an attempt in that direction.

This book was written last year in the Rawalpindi jail when I was undergoing imprisonment under the Defense of India Rules. It could not see the light of day, as I had to proceed rather hurriedly to Karachi to recuperate from my shattered health. Even now, its publication is being rushed through, and I found practically no opportunity to go through the proofs.

I'm most grateful to my young friend, Mr. Abdullah Butt, for the invaluable help he has rendered in looking through the proofs. I would not be exaggerating if I say that it would have been delayed still further but for his untiring energy and enthusiasm.

Lastly, I have to make an appeal to the general reader to appreciate the outlook and the viewpoint that has been impressed in this book and ignore its faults. I hope that my sincere voice, though feeble, shall have the desired effect.

Karachi (Ch.) **AFZAL HAQ.**

15 May, 1941.

The Problem

M r. Jinnah, like a ruthless terrorist, has thrown a bomb amidst us, creating chaos and confusion at a time when concerted action was our greatest need. The ultra-nationalist Jinnah has turned into a rank communalist. It must set us [to] thinking. The League resolution, which was passed at his insistence [clearly] aiming at the vivisection of this country into two parts, may be condemned as ill-timed, if not wholly mischievous, and it reveals a sure sign of a serious ailment in the body politic of India. As clever a politician as he is, he has taken full advantage of the present strained relations of the two major communities. Instead of applying the balm to heal the wounds, he has thought it fit to apply the knife to cut the body into pieces. It's just possible that the Muslim League leaders may not be serious in carrying the Lahore Resolution to its logical conclusion, but the ball is set rolling, and no one should be in doubt as to the serious consequences that will accrue from it. The slogan of a separate Muslim nation is bound to create a deep impression on the Muslim masses. No one can easily call a halt to the [separatist] tendencies of Muslim capitalists. Muslim masses are completely in the hands of the [capitalist class]. The tendencies manifested by the upper [class] are bound to capture the imagination of the Muslim community as a whole. It can unfortunately be concluded that the present differences will be accentuated so much that the past communal disturbances will pale in significance when compared to future upheavals. The partition scheme of Mr. Jinnah is not stillborn; on the contrary, the League has given birth to a many-headed monster that is capable of doing immense harm if not properly controlled. The question of questions is how to control the baffling situation created by the League resolution. My answer to this is that we should dispassionately analyze the forces behind that demand and know the causes of the trouble before suggesting the remedy for it.

The world today is amazed at how the Nazi Leaders built up their power on an absurd theory of Aryan superiority and how the most advanced nation in Europe meekly accepted the leadership of the so-called uncultured Hitler. The communal history is absolutely relevant to the problem with which we have to deal [with] in India. High-sounding statements and unnecessary platitudes will bear no result. They will rather worsen the situation. There is no denying the fact that communalism existed even before the advent of the British Raj and after [India's] domination by the foreigners. Our national leaders did not try to take a realistic view of the situation, with the result that the situation practically went out of their hands. I admit quite frankly that our leaders tried to grapple with the political problems of the country very earnestly from time to time, but not very intelligently.

We always tried to rest in the comfortable belief that the Muslim masses clamor for some political rights and that there is no other problem that immediately confronts them. That erroneous conclusion led the leaders to tackle the communal problem from the wrong end. The communal problem is at once a political, religious, historical, social, and economic one. The political aspect is the least significant. The religious side of the question is given undue importance. Social and economic aspects of the question have been neglected altogether. This neglect of the all-important phase of our lives is responsible for the wrong lead given by the League. Why does the cry uttered by the [separatists] gather strength? It is because the Muslim masses are swayed by anti-Hindu passions. Again comes the question, "Why is it so?" My analysis of the problem will not be agreeable to the Hindus, and the fundamentals of my solution cannot be palatable to the Muslim Leaguers, but I courageously claim that my reading of the situation is 80 percent correct, and the remedy suggested by me is 80 percent correct. I know that the ultranationalists and the rank communalists will give a cold reception to this book. But wide circulation and universal approbation is not [my aim]. My only object is to educate the moderate elements of all communities in the country as to the real problem that confronts us.

Hitler's theory of race superiority may look like a huge joke to us, but there is a hard rock of grievances behind it. The Versailles Treaty not only pronounced the verdict of political serfdom on the German people, but they were relentlessly robbed and looted economically as well. I am sure that you would swoon with horror if you knew a quarter of the misery of the German people after the treaty. The learned author of *The Fool Hath Said* says, "The streets of Berlin before the Nazi regime, when everybody was for sale, when hunger drove boys and girls to submit themselves to revolting humiliations, when the wildest whim of the most erotic taste could be gratified for the payment of a few marks." So it was not the slogan of Hitler that worked wonders in the Naziland, but it was the misery of the masses that brought the Germans under his banner. Passions can only be aroused when there is a genuine grievance and a solid demand for redress behind it. Slogans are the outward manifestation of a grievous wrong to a community. Sometimes demands are manifestly exaggerated, and the arguments supporting them very faulty; still, foolish slogans are more effective than a well-worded sermon, provided there is reasonable cause for complaint.

Mr. Jinnah may be manifestly wrong in his arguments, but the very fact that the Muslim masses are carried away by the slogan of a separate Muslim nation is conclusive proof of the fact that they bear some genuine grievances that ought to be remedied at once. I admit that passions can be worked up in unintelligent people for a short period. But the masses cannot be led away by clever people for all times unless there is a real cause for complaint.

The late Lala Lajpat Raj, a very charming and intelligent leader of the Punjab, and joining hands with the Pandit Madan Mohan Malviji, started to rouse the passions of the Hindu community in the year 1926. A Pathan invasion and Muslim domination were their slogans. These two gentlemen had a long record of service to their country and community. Their forceful communal speeches turned the scales in favor of the Hindu Maha Sabha. Congressional candidates were completely routed at the polling booth. Most prominent congressmen forfeited their securities in the general elections of 1926. Hindu masses sided with Lalaji and Panditji and betrayed the Congress throughout upper India. When the election fever was over, the Hindu masses regained their lost balance. There was absolutely no danger of a Pathan invasion; hence, the Hindu masses thought that they were [misled], and since then, they have refused to accept the wrong lead of the Hindu Maha Sabha. The Muslim dominance through an Afghan invasion was a mere bogey, and so the Hindu masses could not be duped forever by that bogus slogan. The result was that Hindu Maha Sabha leaders looked small in the eyes of their own people, and the Congress emerged strong from this conflict. Contrary to that, Muslim capitalist and communalist leaders had always been successful in turning the Muslim masses around their little fingers. Instead of wasting time in finding out the fundamental mistakes in Mr. Jinnah's reasoning, I now try to diagnose the malady and prescribe a recipe for it.

I will not quarrel with those who argue that the Muslim masses are more prone to base suggestions than those of any other community, but I refuse to believe that this state of affairs is the creation of passion only and that Muslims fly at Hindu threats without rhyme or reason. It is just possible that the personal reason may be missing, but surely there are communal reasons for taking each other by the throat. We must either try to appreciate each other's difficulties and resolve to solve them or submit to the inevitable.

2

Religion

I t would give the best cause for headache to those who might like to know what is meant by the term "nation," but it will be a complacent self-deception to say without an intimate knowledge of Indian life whether Indian people constitute a nation or not. Generally speaking, the term is applied to a people who have common descent, common language, common history, and common religion, but to make the term more comprehensive and up-to-date, add three more items: (1) common social customs, (2) common political institutions, and (3) common economic conditions.

It is admitted on all hands that the majority of Musalmans in this country are direct descendants of those Aryan invaders who in the obscurity of prehistoric times pressed downward through the northwest passes and settled in India. The descendants of the Mughal, Pathan, and Arab invaders are few and far between. Hence, if untold blessings are inherent in the fact of one nationality, and if nationality depends on common blood, then Hindus and Muslims ought not to lead a cat-and-dog life as they do at present. The long and short of the matter is that prejudices that are rampant in this country like a mad lion are not due to racial hatred, and we must search for their causes somewhere else. Is this, then, the difference of religion that has made us a nation at war with itself? Many will cry ditto to it with unshakable certainty, but I politely refuse to believe it, though that refusal may shake their long-standing belief. It is one of the ironies of history that Islam and Hinduism, in spite of highly tolerant teachings, by a series of accidents, should have become unfit for enforcing tolerance on their followers. There is nothing inherently wrong in the teachings of either religion. They teach us to live in peace and serve each other to the best of our abilities. It is not religion but other revolutionary [urges] that are responsible for the present state of affairs.

The very fact that Sanatanist Hindus believe in a world soul called Brahma, who includes everything and in whom everything is included, makes the Hindu religion as great as the world soul. To a Sanatanist Hindu, therefore, this apparent divergence in the religious belief is the least objectionable. To him, this apparent conflict between contrary creeds is a *Lila* (or *Tamasha*) of *Bhagwan* (God). Everyone is ordained to play [their] part well in the world theatre without taking anything to heart. In every man who seeks to serve others, he sees the *rup*, manifestation of Bhagwan, and he will call him *devta*, the compassionate. Whoever by tact and art rises to fame and position is an incarnation of God. Rama and Krishna on account of great military feats are worshipped as God's incarnations. One Vedanta philosophy fully supports and encourages this belief.

The *Bhagwat Gita*, or "the song of the Blessed One," admits the realization of truth from diverse points of view. Intolerance is thus rooted out, and petty prejudices are washed off from the mind. A Hindu is, in fact, a gentleman who never inflicts pain on others and who is tender toward everybody. On account of Vedanta philosophy, he becomes patient, forbearing, and resigned. You can attack Hinduism on other grounds, but no one can deny the fact, so far as his religious ethics goes, that a Hindu does not assign any great importance to one's religious belief for *mokhsa* or *nirvana* (salvation). You may believe in Brahma, Vishnu, Shiva, and Indra, or you may abuse them. You may believe in the Vedas, or you may criticize the books. Put your faith in puranas or refuse to believe in them. In Hinduism, it is all the same. Hinduism has absolutely no quarrel with other faiths. On his way to the temple, a Hindu will have no objection to bowing before the tomb of a Muslim saint. He will touch a Ta'zia with reverence. He will not kill an enemy. On the contrary, he will be hospitable enough to offer milk to a serpent that happens to make its appearance in his house. Hindu religion is admittedly a peace-loving religion.

Islam is the religion of peace. A Muslim is no doubt a soldier of God, but he has to submit himself to His will. The erroneous idea that a soldier cannot be a good peacemaker and lover of peace is responsible for depicting Islam as a militant religion. Islam is rigid only in enforcing certain articles of faith, but for those outside its pale, it has no other message but that of goodwill and tolerance. The rigidity of the private religious duties of the Muslim is looked upon as an act of bigotry by those who do not think like him [or her]. Islam suffered at the hands of those critics who studied it to show its defects rather than appreciate its beauties.

In Islam, race or origin is neither a handicap nor a privilege. It aims at forming a classless society; so, its doctrines are best suited to the proletariat. It urges people not to be aggressive.

The Quran says:
Let there be no compulsion
In religion; Truth stands out
Clear from error: Whoever
Rejects Evil and believes
In God hath grasped
The most trustworthy
Handhold, that never breaks
And God heareth
And knoweth all things.

As a Muslim, you may invite people to the fold of Islam, but you cannot use harsh words, not to speak of forceful conversion. The Book [Quran] says:
Invite all to the Way
Of thy Lord with wisdom
And beautiful preaching;
And argue with them
In ways that are best
And most gracious.

A true Muslim is further forbidden to speak ill of deities and gods of other religions:
Revile not ye
Those whom they call upon

7

Besides God; lest
They out of spite
Revile God
In their ignorance.

After the Quran, Muslims respect the sayings of the Prophet most. It is said that Abdullah, son of Omar, a companion of the Prophet, slaughtered a goat. There was a Jew living in his neighborhood. He asked his wife whether she had sent a portion of it to the Jewish neighbor or not. She answered in the negative. Abdullah said, "Send him a portion at once," because he had heard from the Prophet that the Angel Gabriel impressed upon him to do good to his neighbors so insistently that the Prophet sometimes thought that God would send an order to all believers to bequeath their property to neighbors as well.

It must be borne in mind that, in accordance with good treatment to one's neighbors, Islam does not make any distinction between a Muslim and a non-Muslim.

Abu Hurairah, another companion of the Prophet, said that he had heard from the lips of the Prophet, "He whose neighbors are not immune from mischief shall not enter Paradise."

The Prophet further said, "You shall not be Musalmans unless you learn to love your neighbors." There is another saying to the same effect. "If you wish that God and His apostle might love you, then serve your neighbors."

There are hundreds of such sayings that go to show that Islam has the greatest respect for a neighbor, whether Muslim or non-Muslim. The Prophet ordered Muslims to treat a non-Muslim relative kindly and help him in his needs. The faithful are allowed to take a non-Muslim wife, and the wife is allowed to retain her religion and social customs.

To do justice in a neutral atmosphere is not difficult, but the real test comes when a man has to do justice to the people who hate him or for whom he has an aversion. Whatever the circumstances, a Muslim is required to abide by the highest moral law. The Book of Islam says:

O, ye who believe!
Stand out firmly
For God as witness
To fair dealings and let not

The hatred of others
To you make you swerve
To wrong, and depart from
Justice. Be just! That is
Next to piety; and fear God
For God is well acquainted
With all that you do.

It is clear beyond all doubt that it is not religion but religious insincerity that has made this land hell on earth. All agitation against religion must cease because both Hinduism and Islam teach love and not hatred. Let us with one voice protest against those who in the name of religion do irreligious acts.

I quite agree that the central fact of the teachings of Islam is different from that of Hinduism. According to Islam, God sends down prophets, but does not take any shape or form Himself, whereas the reverse is the case with Hinduism. However, as time passed on, new theories and conclusions were mixed up with the religious beliefs of Islam. Some mystics changed the whole phase of this religion and brought it more in agreement with the Vedanta theory of the Sanatanist Hindus. Puritans may enter the strongest protest against this attempt of the Sufis, but the fact is that in spite of these protestations, Sufism is now the accepted religion of 80 percent of the Muslims in India. The mystic theory of the Sufis is in consonance with the Vedanta theory; therefore, Musalman masses in religious practices resemble Hindus. If Hindus bow down before an image of a deity, Muslims bow down before the graves of saints and pirs. Islam prohibits music and dance, but in every khanqah, you hear sweet music and see elegant dancing. You will further see some of the religious leaders of the masses themselves dancing in ecstasy, and they are so carried away by the music and dance of the prostitutes that folds of their turbans become loose, and they weep and cry like little children. Ordinary prostitutes have taken the place of Ðev Dasis in the shrines of Muslim Sufis. Music and dance are now as much a part of the Muslim religion as they are in Hinduism. The question of music before mosques is absolutely a political stunt. Daily, I see and hear dance and music before the mosques near the shrines of Muslim saints and pirs. No one takes objection to it. Whoever dares to protest against it does it at the risk of his [or her] life.

If a Muslim of the first century of the hijra were again sent down to this earth to see the state of religious affairs in India, he [or she] would at once say that 80 percent of the Muhammadans inhabiting India are *Kafirs* and that they have only adopted the name of Muslim to gain their political ends. Otherwise, there is absolutely no religious difference between the Hindus and the so-called Muslims. A living pir and a dead saint are revered more than a prophet by the ignorant masses. God is dethroned, and the prophet is installed instead. Here are some of the poems that are generally recited by musicians and dancing girls at the shrines of great Muslim saints and Sufis and appreciated by audiences.

Allah has nothing in His skirt except His "Oneness":

اللہ کے پاس میں وحدت کے سوا کیا ہے ۔ ۔

جو کچھ ہمیں لینا ہے لے لیں گے محمد سے ۔

We will get whatever we desire from Muhammad.

جو مستوی تھا سر عرش پر خدا ہو کر ۔
اتر پڑا ہے مدینہ میں مصطفیٰ ہو کر ۔

He who had been sitting as God on the ninth heaven has come down to Medina in the human form of Mustafa, the Prophet.

کل تو مندر میں برا ہمن کو دیتے تھے درشن ۔
آج مسجد میں مسلمان بنے بیٹھے ہیں ۔

Yesterday you showed your face to the Brahmin in the temple; Today you appear as a Muslim in the Mosque.

مكهـد سر وحـدت هـے كوئى يـه رمز كـيا جـانـے -
شريعـت مين تو بنـده هـے حقيقتـا مين خـدا جـانـے -

Muhammad is the secret of Oneness. Who is there who can understand this nice point? According to the apparent law of Islam, he is a human being, but what he is in reality is known to God alone.

It is not the Prophet alone that looks like God to Musalmans nowadays, but true to Vedanta theory, every head of the Mystic Order is looked upon as God in human form.

چاچـر وانگ مدينـر دـے كوٹ مٹـهـن بيـتـا اللـه -
ظاهر دـے وچ پـهر فريدن باطـن دـے وچ اللـه -

Chachar (the last resting place of the saint) looks like Medina (the place where the body of the Prophet is interred).

Pir Faridan is a human being in appearance, but in fact he is Allah.

براكـے چشـم بيـنـا أز مدينـم بر سر ملتـان -
بشـكل صـدر دين خـود رحمـت للعالمين آمـد -

For those who have the eye to see, (Khan Bahadur) Sadr Din of Multan (a pir) is the Prophet Muhammad himself who has come from Medina to Multan.

Hear friend, that gay Lord has taken the human form.

سن کرے پرنگی مولا بن آیا ناسوتی ہے ۔
احد نہیں بن احمد آیا ایہہ ملنگ بھجھوتی ہے ۔

This "Hermit" who has applied dust to his body is in fact Ahad (God), but he has now come incarnated as Ahman (the Prophet).

This is a bird's-eye view of the religious convictions that influence the Muslim masses. Such mystic expressions were formerly confined to *khanqahs* (monasteries) alone, but in the mosques, the differences were maintained between the creator and the created. Now mysticism or Vedanta theory has taken possession of the pulpits as well. I have seen a band of musicians reciting such allegorical poems to the people dancing round the pulpit of a famous mosque of Shah Mohammad Ghaus outside Delhi Gate, Lahore. The following couplets are inscribed on the inner walls of the Jama Mosque of Garshankar.

بنده از بندگی خدا گردد ۔
نتواند کہ مصطفیٰ گردد ۔

"By worshipping, the worshipper becomes God, but he cannot become Mustafa (the Prophet)."

قطرہ در آب رفتہ آب شود   نتواند کہ در ناب شود ۔

("A drop of water mixing with water becomes water, but cannot become a pearl.")

No one can now dare to raise a finger in protest against such sentiments, [as being] absolutely against the teachings of Islam. Whoever does, he [or she] will do so at the risk of his life. The body of the great puritan leader Mujaddid Ahmad of Sarhind, who fought his whole life against the corrupt ceremonies, was buried after his death without any [tombstone] on the grave. After three centuries, his followers have now taken it into their heads to raise a great sepulchral monument over the buried body of their master; the puritans have always looked down upon those who raised any building over the dead body of any person. Now mysticism has captured the imagination of the Muslim masses, and they are favorably inclined toward Hindu practices. This learning process toward Hinduism would have been more rapid but for the Arya Smaj propaganda. However, it is clear from the prevalent customs of Musalmans and the rapid growth of khanqahs that the religious beliefs of Hindus and Muslims are not poles asunder as some people are apt to believe. In spite of Sufism and Vedanta theories being the guiding principles of Muslims and Hindus respectively, their relations are more strained than before. Though Islam in India has absolutely taken the color of Hinduism, the communal disturbances are looked upon as if they were only due to religious differences.

Some of those who cast a momentary look at the events will try to challenge my assertion that the learning process toward Hinduism would have been more rapid but for the Arya Smaj. It is my firm belief that if Swami Dyanand, the great scholar and well-wisher of the Hindus, had not come to the rescue of Islam, the 20 percent of puritans that now exist could never have managed to survive. Before the anti-Muslim preaching of Smaj leaders, the Muslim masses had been absolutely devoid of any religious fervor, and they were about to lose their individuality in Hindu society as untouchables. But the virulent Arya Smaj propaganda against Islam whipped some of the Muslim theologians into activity, who took the first opportunity to establish Arabic schools in different parts of the country. They raised the slogan of "down with the Hindu customs" with success. Hindu and Muslim masses were divided into two different war camps for the first time. In politics, Muslims definitely leaned toward Britishers. Though they had not much religious fervor left in them, they recovered a little from apathy and began to think as a separate entity. I do not deny the fact that the "divide and rule" policy of the government is also responsible for the present estranged relations, but the anti-Hindu passions in the Muslim masses were greatly aroused by the ruthless mass attack of the Arya Smaj on Islam. Musalmans of India, though Musalmans in name, still called themselves Musalmans. The unskillful and unabated propaganda of the Smaj throughout the length and breadth of Upper India made an adverse effect on the Muslim classes, and the Muslim masses were unconsciously carried away by the *esprit de corps*. The result was that the Muslim masses, though they knew little of Islam, became anti-Hindu, and the Hindu also imbibed an anti-Muslim passion in those parts of the country where the Arya Smaj was the strongest.

Those puritans who entered into defensive war against the Arya Smaj, in the heart of their hearts, were thankful to the Arya Smaj because its propaganda afforded them the opportunities of playing the party game with passion and of easily bringing the Muslim masses to their side, if not of religiously reforming them to their satisfaction. The Arya Smaj raised the cry of "Hindus in danger" at a time when Hinduism was gaining a victory over Islam. The political power of the Musalmans was gone, and there was no driving force left in them. Sanatana Dharma, being based on Vedanta theory, is an ocean-wide religion. Islam, like a stream, was about to lose its identity in Sanatana Dharma's water when the Arya Smaj succeeded in parting Hindus and Musalmans in watertight compartments. Smajists claim that they had reformed the Hindus and saved them from becoming Muslims or Christians. But what is the Arya Smaj? It is the Hindi edition of Islam declaring a crusade against everything that was held sacred by Hindus. That was the religious aspect of it. Its belated attempts to protect Hindus from the onslaughts of Islam had absolutely no spiritual significance. Islam at that time was in a morbid condition when the great Swami conceived the idea of saving Hindus from becoming Musalmans. It is just possible that Swami might have seen some people engaged in a futile attempt to take a small bucket of water from the deep ocean of Hindu society, but he failed to see that the stream of Islam was falling into that deep ocean and fast losing its identity. Those who ignore the assimilating power of Hinduism are fools. Sanatana Dharma apparently looks stupid and unemotional, but it is obstinate beyond comprehension, and therein [lies] its strength. Hinduism was about to devour the whole of Muslim society as it devoured Buddhism and Jainism, but the Shuddhi cry of the Smaj made Musalmans alert. I always appreciate the benevolent attempts of the Arya Smaj in the field of education, but its religious efforts helped the Musalmans to realize their separate [identity], become stubborn in politics, and, at the same time, de-Hinduize the Hindus more than any other movement. For all intents and purposes, the Arya Smaj defeated its own end.

The Religious philosophy of the Arya Smaj is akin to the teachings of original Islam. Smajists are religiously more aggressive than Musalmans so far as the disrespect of Hindu gods and idols is concerned. Mysticism and the Vedanta theory are quite identical, and mysticism is the religion of 80 percent of the Muslim masses, who have drifted a long way from the Islam of Arabia. In spite of these facts, there are Hindu-Muslim clashes but no Sanatanist Arya disturbances. All these facts go to show that our differences are not religious, but that these estranged relations are based on other justified feelings of being wronged.

Sikhism, another great movement, ought to be studied in this connection. This movement was essentially a spiritual principle and had no political application, and in the beginning, on account of a series of incidents, it developed into a political movement and became anti-Muslim in color and character. As far as its religious philosophy is concerned, it is still a Gurmukhi edition of Islam, believing in one God, despising idolatry, and even speaking of the Prophet with respect. Though Sikhs claimed to be a separate community politically and their saints were not immune from the virulent attacks of the Smajists, there was hardly any clash between Hindus and Sikhs or between Sikhs and Smajists on so large a scale as between Hindus and Muslims. Though there is a great religious resemblance between Sikhism and Islam, there is no love lost between the two in the daily conduct of life. The sympathies of the Sikhs are invariably on the side of Hindus, and Hindus always side with Sikhs when any quarrel arises over a social or political matter.

When I see that in spite of the fact that present-day Islam in India is an Arabic version of Sanatana Dharma, and in spite of the fact that Sikhism and Arya Smaj are respectively more or less Gurmukhi and Hindi editions of original Islam, and still there is animosity between Hindus and Muslims, and Sikhs and Smajists always side with Hindus, I come to the reasonable conclusion that the Hindu-Muslim problem is not a religious one, and that we must find out those causes that are responsible for the present state of affairs in the country.

It is a familiar but fallacious notion that only Sufis are tolerant toward others and that puritan Mullah are bigoted beyond redemption. The Mullah is no doubt conservative to the core, but all Mullahs will rise with one accord against those who will be tyrannical toward others in any way. The term *Kafir* has nothing nauseous in it. These religious scholars have to use this term to differentiate a Musalman from a non-Muslim. The non-believers, or Kafirs, may have their retribution in the next world, but as citizens they are not worse off. Islam does not throw Kafirs to the wolves; it rather throws a shield over them. A Mullah, in fact, is he who can afford to be harsh and intolerant toward the believers, but he has no option but to be kind toward Kafirs. Among his own community, he is a police officer always to be dreaded. For those outside the pale of Islam, he has a message of goodwill and peace. It is the cosmopolitan Muslims who depicted him as a frowning demon; in fact, he is a smiling deity who always thinks well and wishes good for others, and more especially for Kafirs.

I quite realize that a Hindu friend will look askance at me because he has never heard anything favorable and kind about a Mullah, but I have convincing proof to change his opinion. The Jamiat-ul-Ulema is a body consisting of religious scholars only. You will always find them fighting on the side of the Congress and explaining away the inconsistencies of the congressmen even at the risk of being dubbed hirelings of the Hindus. Who is Mauiana Abul Kalam Azad? A religious scholar of great renown. It is his religiosity that stimulates him not only to take an active part in politics, but also to always defend Congress and Hindu friends from the onslaughts of the unkind Muslim critics.

There is another Muslim organization called the Majlis-i-Ahrar. This is a proletarian organization. Its leadership is in the hands of those who are religious-minded people. They are more favorably inclined toward the Hindus and always preach forbearance toward their non-Muslim neighbors. Those Muslim Leagues and societies which have no religious background, not only off and on, but constantly, kick up a row against the Hindus and the Congress. Are not these facts sufficient to revise one's opinion about the Mullahs and exclaim with one accord that our present differences have nothing to do with religion?

Take note of another fact. There are two Muslim Universities, one at Aligarh and the other at Deoband. The former imparts secular knowledge, and the latter is a center of religious learning. The mentality of Aligarh students is always pro-British and anti-Hindu, but the mentality of Deoband scholars is anti-British and pro-Congress. The leadership of the Muslim League is in the hands of those who are students of the Aligarh College or other English universities. They have little or no knowledge of Islam as compared with the members of the Jamiat-ul-Uleman. Had our differences been due to religion, then the Jamiat-ul-Ulema and the Majlis-i-Ahrar would have been more vociferous than the League in decrying the Congress and the Hindus. Last, but not least, had the present complications something to do with religion, then Muslims could not be led by Mr. Jinnah, an able lawyer and politician, but admittedly the last Musalman on earth to know anything of Islam.

UNTOUCHABILITY

The meek and non-militant Hindu, who is very broad-minded in religion, at once turns around with his tail up if he enters the social field. He changes color and begins to show his teeth if you dare to go near him. If a Muslim aristocrat in a princely dress goes to a Hindu confectioner to buy some sweetmeats, he has to stand at a respectable distance or he has to get a stern rebuke from the shopkeeper. Dare a Muslim touch the confectioner's hand when giving him the price? No, he has to stretch out his hand with palm up to receive the sweetmeats that will be thrown from some height by the confectioner so that his body may not be polluted by the touch of the Muslim customer. A Hindu is otherwise a thorough gentleman, but his small-mindedness in the social field touches the Muslim community to the quick. I am sure that it is not out of spite that Hindus adopt this attitude. Their attitude toward the Musalman is the natural corollary of their social system, and they never dream that anybody would take objection to it. There are certain sections of people among the Muslim community that feel the sting of it and openly say that the Hindus aim to destroy them, and they will make full attempts to rob them of their self-respect at every step. To those who do not think with me in this respect, I say that we differ as to the motive of the Hindu, but I am not in doubt as to the effect on the Muslim community. Self-respect and a fine sense of becoming are no doubt killed in a man who does not resent such treatment. An inferiority complex is developed in those who are

17

so treated. Off and on, I try to make provisions for my sweepers to dine with me, but as a class, the harijans have developed an inferiority complex, and they never agree to it unless and until threatened or compelled. Very recently, I asked a harijan convict in this jail to dine with me. Hearing this, he ran away and hid himself in the latrine. Two other convicts dragged him out and made him sit on a blanket near me. His hands were washed, and I gave him a spoon. He was trembling from head to foot as if he had been suffering from shaking palsy for a long time. I was taking a dish made of rice and split pulses. He took a spoonful of it, and putting it on the palm of his hand, he threw it in his mouth, taking care that the spoon might not touch his lips. He dared not sit face-to-face with me. He turned his back on me with his eyes downcast as if a Hindu bride in a conservative family sitting in front of her husband was performing a *gauna* ceremony. After taking three or four mouthfuls, he fled again to take shelter in the latrine. To partake of my food was a great ordeal for [him]. He told a friend that five minutes of that evening looked like five years of [trial] to him. This goes to show how we have taken the life out of them and crushed their self-respect. They cannot now feel a heartbeat for deeper things. They cannot understand the real significance of the struggle for freedom and its true motivating force.

Do the Musalmans ill-treat the untouchable out of spite? No, Hindus and Musalmans both quite innocently inflict poisoned stings on our countrymen, the untouchables. A serpent can take life out of a man, but we kill the man in the untouchable. A lion preys upon the beasts without remorse, so do we treat the untouchables, without [remorse], for the wrongs [they never] committed. Though the element of ill will is absent in our treatment of them, the harm done to them is incalculable. The great heart of our people will not weigh down with grief unless and until God sends down a leader for the untouchables who would courageously revolt against the existing state of affairs and organize the harijans so as to knock down those who discriminate unfairly between man and man under the influence of wealth, caste, creed, or occupation. He must be a curious creature who would dare to call harijans an integral part of the Indian nationhood. Unless we break sharply with our social system and customs and treat the harijans as our own kith and kin, we cannot improve our lot as a nation. If the similarity of geographical and political conditions makes the people a nation, then we Indians are a nation no doubt, but the truth of the matter is that we have been divided into factions since 1857 and ready to subjugate, if not to consume each other. Untouchability is the first essential cause of our division, and consequently our weakness. Some optimistic people say that our revolutionary [zeal] will solve the knotty question. India is too deeply rooted in traditions and will not easily weather the storm of any political change. Only social revolution, which is essentially based on economic justice, can make a favorable change in the lot of the people. Otherwise, to all intents and purposes, this country will remain a house divided against itself for a long time to come. Islam was the greatest socially leveling movement, but it has failed to achieve its end in India, and the Musalmans themselves were absorbed into the caste system.

The old Indian life not only survived the shock of Islam, but it also endured the new Western ideas. Indians have not seen a marked change in their social system even after the advent of the British Raj in India. The efforts of a few broad-visioned Hindus did not bring a desired change in the mentality of the masses.

I am conscious of the fact that there was no constant head breaking before the arrival of the British people in this country. That was because there was no occasion for that. The Musalmans continued to be treated as untouchables since their first invasion of the soil right up to the Congress regime. Musalmans remained an army of occupation in a hostile population for a thousand years. This gave them political authority and prestige. The Hindus treated the Musalmans as untouchables, and the Musalmans treated them as a subject race. Both were satisfied and comfortable in their own societies. The idea of one nation was absolutely absent from their minds. Rajput princes and Mughal emperors cooperated with each other in the field of politics, but the Hindu-Muslim masses did not constitute a nation even then. Akbar, like a great Sufi, enlarged the boundaries of faith. But even this expansion of the realm of religion did not bring about the desired result. So far as the masses were concerned, politics was the concern of the [Hindu and Muslim upper] classes only. Though [the Hindu and Muslim upper] classes made peace among themselves, the masses did not come near each other. Untouchability still divided them into different and hostile camps.

As I have already stated, the Musalmans were not treated as untouchables out of spite but because untouchability was part of Indian life from time immemorial, and no Manu was alive to assign the Musalmans to a fifth caste in the Hindu society. Brahma had already given birth to Brahman from his mouth, Kshatriya from his shoulder, Vaisya from his thigh, and lowly Sudras from his feet; there was hardly any part of the body left to allot to the new class of people. Those who have no class must go to the lowest one, Sudras [the untouchable class]; the invaded and Malech as [Muslims], were looked upon as people of one class because they could not dream of any other class. The Musalmans did not meddle with the social system of the Hindus and only contented themselves with snatching political power from their hands. After the collapse of the Mughal Empire, the Musalmans bowed low before the British people. After the loss of political power and prestige, untouchability remained the chief legacy of Islam in India. Though Muslims lived side by side with Hindus for centuries, this long association failed to produce a sensible fusion between the two peoples. After losing the empire, the Muslims suddenly felt that they were standing on the lowest rung of the social ladder. The loss of the empire was not a material loss to the vast masses of the Muslim community because the history of Islam in India is the history of kings and [empires], and they had no voice in the administration of the country. However, they lost the doubtful prestige and happiness of being of the same faith as the Emperor.

For some years of the Christian rule, the Muslim masses were quite satisfied with their lot of being untouchables of the Hindus and Serfs of the British Government, and in fact there was no energy left in them. The new system of British Government generated a new force in the Hindu intelligentsia, and they imbibed new ideas and thoughts of the West. Although the magnificent edifice of the British administration in India was constructed on the ruins of the despotic Mughal Empire, it had a democratic background, and the right of citizenship was recognized even for the man in the street. In spite of the fact that every collector and deputy commissioner was a miniature Mughal emperor in some way, still there was a spirit of respect for individual liberty prevalent in the administration. The Hindu classes welcomed the new era, and with the help of large-hearted Englishmen, formed the political organization known as the Indian National Congress to demand more rights in the name of the people. Though this new era was looked on with suspicion by the religious section of the Muslim community, the classes soon declared their loyalty toward the British Crown, and the masses only opened their eyes to survey the change. They thought that the fates had played false with them and that their case was now hopeless. Through the incessant Congress propaganda, Indians became conscious of their entity for the first time in history. The Muslim masses were still in a dormant condition. The British Government, as a counterblast to the Congress claims, began to organize loyal Muslims into Megentia of the upper stratum of the Muslim community, and the Arya Smaj exasperated the religious section. Both the vocal sections among the Musalmans began to spur the inactive masses. Politics did not interest the Muslim rank and file. "Religion in danger" had also no meaning to them because there was little or no difference between Hindu Dharma and the Islam of India. However, the social treatment of Hindus excited them to anger. Though this treatment was not a new phenomenon, this era of individual liberty brought about a little consciousness in the Muslim masses. They were dormant, but not dead. The British efforts in the field of politics and Arya Smaj activities in the field of religion excited anti-Hindu passions in the Muslim masses. The Muslim Intelligentsia and the puritan Musalmans played an important part in creating this strong feeling. Musalmans of the Aryan race, Musalmans of the Sufi cult, Musalmans of the High Houses, and Musalmans of good education were treated alike as untouchables by the Hindu Society. You may be a *pucca* nationalist and foursquare Gandhi-ite, but you will be treated as an untouchable as soon as you announce to a Hindu that you are a Musalman. However justified the Hindus feel and however innocent they plead in their treatment of the Musalmans, in justice they cannot blame their counterparts if they cultivate an ill feeling toward them.

I do not insist on a change of heart because the heart of the Hindus is not impure, and a great majority of them treat the Musalman as such without any ill feeling. But it can be rightly said that this single practice goes to show to the world that Indians are not one people and that Mr. Jinnah is justified in raising the flag of separation.

My own little story will convey a lesson and shed light on the subject. While still a minor, I was asked to get some curd from the bazaar. In my anxiety to be looked upon as a clever boy, I did not buy it from the shop near at hand. I went a little farther, hoping that I would get fresh curd and so deserve the smiles of my mother. In those days, there was hardly any Muslim *halvai* throughout the city of Amritsar. Hindu and Sikh confectioners did not even receive money from the Muslim customer in their hands lest his touch should pollute them. For this purpose, they always used a wooden ladle—the Hindu shopkeeper holding the handle while the Muslim customer was asked to put cash money in the cup [or] bowl. This wooden *doi* was in use because wood is considered a nonconductor, and a Hindu shopkeeper's purity was saved from being destroyed by means of this contrivance. Unfortunately, when putting the price in the bowl of the ladle, my wrist touched its edge. The man became a demon, and he hurled a thousand filthy abuses at me. For a moment I was stunned and stood motionless before departing, never to visit a Hindu or Sikh confectioner's shop in the later years of my life. This simple incident that changed the social aspect of my life took place when there was no political and social agitation in the country, and Muhammadans were used to pocketing such insults daily. To my knowledge, the first cry of the boycott of Hindu shops was effectively raised in the city of Gujrat (Punjab). The Paisa Akhbar was the only weekly organ of the Musalmans in those days; it fanned the flames, and the movement spread like fire. It seemed that Muslims were only too eager to receive the message because the princes and the people both had their own sad experiences of the Hindu treatment. Muslim shops were opened, but for any constructive program, economic stability is necessary. The Musalman is lacking in this respect. The result was that the bubble burst soon, and 90 percent of the shops were closed down. The age-long traditions have made the Hindus too conservative to change under any pressure. The Hindu leaders have up to this time displayed a noble vagueness toward this all-important question. The result is that after the defensive Gujrat boycott movement, which was spontaneous, other organized efforts followed in its trail. Some Musalmans in their attempt to save themselves from the social tyranny of the Hindus have unfortunately developed an anti-Hindu mania. Muhammadans have not made any rapid stride but have only crawled in the way of removing untouchability.

A few Muslim shops are the only advantage that accrued to the Muslims by this agitation, but its repercussions in politics were immensely harmful. Unsophisticated masses cannot make any distinction between social and political affairs. If once they are upset, their anger knows no limits. In their rage, they even sacrifice their own interests. Here lies the unpopularity of the nationalist leaders. I have heard Sayyid Atta Ullah Shah Bakhari's political lectures. The great speaker carries even the hostile audience with him. In the ecstasy of the moment, the people are so moved that drops of water trickle from their eyes, and they jump to their legs in an excited state of feeling. When this forceful orator says, "Freedom is our birthright. Muslims should get it at all costs," the audience shrieks out in one voice. "Allah is great," they say in approbation. When he says, "But this freedom cannot be attained without Hindu-Muslim unity," the Muslim audience gives him a blank look. "Unity with those," they say, "who treat us as untouchables is an impossible proposition."

In spite of the noble record of sacrifices, a nationalist Musalman is always the loser at the polling booth. Why so? Because, the noble record in the service of the country's freedom to an ordinary Muslim looks [more] like a loyal service to the Hindu cause. The nationalist Musalman accuses the masses of being inert in politics, and the man of the street accuses the nationalist who wants to lead him to be sacrificed at the altar of a Hindu God — Mahatma Gandhi. I know many a noble soul among the Muslims that eagerly joined the forces of freedom but retired brokenhearted because the position of the Muslim masses had been very puzzling. But the key to this puzzle lies in the fact of the social treatment by the Hindu. Early in the khilafat movement, Muslims went to jails in large numbers. At the least, the situation in the Punjab jails was unbearable for Muslim workers, who were undergoing their sentences in "C" class. Hindu and Sikh convicts were in charge of the kitchens, and a Musalman could not dare to pass the threshold. That was not all. Musalmans were ordered to stand at a distance; the Hindu and Sikh convict cooks used to throw loaves of bread at their hands. Then the Muslim political workers had to put the iron cups in rows and retire. The non-Muslim cooks never put cooked vegetables or pulses in the cup that was in the hands of the Muslim because there was the danger of his polluting touch. But the Hindu workers in "C" class were an exception to this rule. As a protest against this treatment, even some prominent Muslim workers in "C" class had to resort to hunger strikes, and they were so unfavorably impressed that, since then, "as you have been done by" is their motto so far as their treatment of the Hindus is concerned.

The immediate effect of this agitation in the Punjab jails was that the government had to arrange for separate kitchens for Muslims. It is quite a curious thing that whenever any social and commercial agitation is started, it always follows or ends in the slogan of "defensive boycott of the Hindu shops". This slogan touches the heart of the people more than anything else. The desire that they should not be treated as untouchables by their Hindu countrymen is ever uppermost in the minds of the Muslim masses. Muslim classes, including the League leaders, always keep aloof from the boycott agitation. They do not act from principle but they keep aloof because they do not feel the pinch of it. Capitalists, whether Hindus, Muhammadans, or Sikhs, do not observe strict boycotts of each other, and Muhammadan capitalists seldom go for shopping in person, and so they do not feel as keenly as the Muslim masses. Moreover, they themselves treat their servants as slaves and outcastes. This defensive boycott of Hindu shops, therefore, is essentially a mass movement. With the awakening of the Muslim masses, the boycott agitation will gain strength and volume.

Unless Hindu leaders bring their influence on the Hindu masses to bear, Hindu-Muslim unity will become a dream. Muslim masses have little to do with politics. They are not politicians who look to the ultimate good of the country. They argue in a very simple way. "Here is our Hindu neighbor who feels polluted by the very touch of our hand. What right has he to feel so? If he has such a right, why should we not pay him in the same coin?". There ends their imagination. I know that a section of the Hindu society wants to see the "touch me not spirit" continue forever, because in this way, a superiority complex is developed in the Hindus, and an inferiority complex is cultivated in the mind of the Musalman. This is a shortsighted view of the situation. Though Islam laughs at the racial or clannish pride, to counteract the Hindu view, Muslims are willfully introducing a new pride based on a false notion of religion that will be ultimately disastrous to the peace of the country. They are using the Hindu ideology to gain their end. They say that a Hindu is a pagan, and therefore polluted; his touch will pollute a Muslim, who is pure in body and soul. According to Islam, all human beings are pure. The religious system of Islam does not rest upon birth, race, or class. Yet, they cleverly use religion to influence their community, because religious hatred is the greatest driving force and therefore an indispensable necessity in this case. Instead of taking up a defensive position and acting upon a constructive program, passions are aroused at once, and the boycott movement ends in Hindu-Muslim clashes. As I have already said, their boycott movements are mass movements without the support of the Muslim capitalists; therefore, they end in a fiasco. Any movement without capital is a body without soul.

A young and smart socialist worker, Sardar Kulbir Singh, brother of the renowned S. Bhagat Singh, asked a very pertinent question while he was with me in Rawalpindi jail. "How is it," he asked, "that no sooner does Ahrar influence increase in a certain locality [then] Hindu shops are closed down and Muslim shops are opened, and the boycott movement gains ground?"

I answered as follows. "Whenever you educate a community politically, it means that you try to revolutionize the whole mentality of the community. You teach them to study the different phases of life themselves; in other words, you ask them to acquire a new sense of dignity and wish of them that they may become alive to the economic miseries all around and feel the pain of humiliation. We continue our lectures to economic exploitation and political serfdom of our people by foreigners, and the people become very touchy on these two points. But when they review the situation and study the position in the light of those lectures, they find the Hindu the worse aggressor than the foreigners in this respect. However clean in person and in dress, he cannot touch a Hindu without defiling him; in some cases, his shadow is pollution for the high caste Hindu. Because he has now acquired a new sense of dignity, he therefore feels the pain of humiliation more than before. Hence, the eruption of the social volcano."

Apparently, this explanation carried weight with him, and he seemed to be favorably impressed by it. Then he said, "The Hindus are themselves in favor of removing this social evil." I told him my impression frankly. "This propaganda against untouchability is a political stunt rather than a change of heart. Hinduism is based on tortuous arrangement of castes. This complicated structure of society is immovable and unprogressive and will continue to refuse any dignities for certain castes and classes. The Hindu as an individual is not only harmless, but a thorough gentleman. When considered in the terms of caste, he is a steamroller that moves slowly but steadily to crush everything that comes in its way. Some noble spirits among the Hindus no doubt cry hoarse against untouchability, but these noble exceptions have not changed the rule of Hindu society so far as the Musalmans are concerned. If today you take the guise of a Musalman in India, you will become sadder and wiser; then and only then will you be able to grasp the problem that puzzles the nationalist Musalmans and pains the Muslim masses."

Then, he related his own adventures in the guise of a Musalman that need not be related, because it is the ordinary lot of a Musalman. To inflict grievous hurt and humiliation is part of the life of a high caste Hindu. It is no part of his program to wreak vengeance, but his action *ipso facto* engenders hate in the hearts of those who are so treated. Here lies the key to the Indian puzzle. The worst part of it is that Hindu parents are still anxious that their sons and daughters should be well up in these superstitions of six thousand years. In the swiftly changing world, you can still see the Hindu ladies coming and going to temples making parabolas and hyperbolas on the road to save the corner of their garment from touching a Muslim passerby. But never think that they are devoid of the human qualities of kindness and compassion. On the contrary, they are the very embodiment of those qualities, but age-long exclusive tradition of family and environment of their society have made them the "touch-me-not."

A Sikh friend of mine asked me why the Muslims were becoming touchier day by day on the question of untouchability while their forefathers had not resented such treatment. I asked him a question, and that was the proper answer to his interrogation. "Why do Indians demand swaraj after a century? The demand for equality of status is inherent in man. Leaders of the campaign of political emancipation of Musalmans and Sudras say this is their natural right, which cannot be long denied or delayed without prejudicing the country's cause." I further told my Sikh friend about how a Hindu lady in my neighborhood had tried to take sweetmeats out from the throat of her minor son, who had unfortunately bought them from a Muslim hawker and gulped them down before she could inform him of the gravity of his action. Several Muslim women witnessed this scene, and in this age of consciousness, such acts go a long way in widening the gulf between the communities instead of paving the way for unity.

I have called the Hindu attempts at removing untouchability a political stunt. I will call Muslim zeal for conversion of the Sudras sheer hypocrisy, because Islam does not condemn any occupation. One's being a street sweeper is no handicap according to Islam. What right has a Muslim to tell a Sudra to embrace Islam before he is treated as a human being? Can he not say, "Physician, heal yourself. Had you been a true Musalman, you would not have put the condition of conversion precedent to my being treated as a son of the soil. You fly into a fit of rage if I come near you. Still you have the audacity of calling me to a religion whose fundamental law is not respected by you."

I know those Musalmans who pose as religious heads, yet they have never tried once in their lives to sit with their house scavengers and invite them to dine with them. But in the pulpit, you will always hear them condemning the caste system of Hindus and praising Islam as a great leveling religion. What hypocrisy! To give oneself out what one is not. They speak like a Musalman no doubt, but they act as a caste-ridden Hindu. If you tell any Muslim religious leader frankly that he is 90 percent Hindu in his religious practice, he will incite someone to take the life out of you. Let us not tell the people what is written in the Quran. Let us act according to its dictation; the world will be eager to follow our religion. Musalmans take great delight in the conversion of great people only and always ignore the underdogs.

It is not only Hinduism that condemned all the members of the Sudra class to the miseries of perpetual untouchability. Musalmans have an equal responsibility for it. All physical and moral instincts are crushed in Sudras. Hindu and Musalmans are equally heartless. To the Sudras, there is no God. If there is any,

He must be deaf or a partisan of the Hindus and Musalmans. If He is just and loving, then why have the Sudras been so mercilessly treated, and why has He never appeared to help them during the last six thousand years? I see Musalmans as heartless as the Hindus, if not more so, in their treatment of Sudras.

The offer of Shuddi by Hindus or conversion by the Musalmans is not to treat a human being as a human being, but to swell their numbers in order that the upper classes of the Musalmans and the high caste Hindus may get political benefit out of them. Hindu congressmen and nationalist Musalmans cry hoarse to get political rights from the government, but I see no change of heart so far as the untouchables are concerned. We have learned to soar high like kites, but we always search for a dead body to feed upon. We use Sudras as a cat's paw to draw chestnuts for us out of the political fires. We have not yet begun to think of Sudras as our countryman and fellow beings. We are only shedding crocodile tears over the lot of the untouchables. We have not yet made up our minds to transform the untouchable into a touchable. We refuse to act upon the religion of Islam and to follow the Prophet in this respect. Musalmans have no message for the untouchables, and consequently Islam does not appeal to them. Musalmans resent the treatment by Hindus, but they never for a minute feel for the Sudras whom they themselves treat in the same way. What injury a man inflicts on a man! No one outside India can comprehend that human nature can be so wicked as it manifests itself in our treatment of the Sudras.

Who can imagine the manifold tyrannies endured by humanity here in this country? A great majority of our people has not a noble soul among them. How often we pass by untouchables without offering to help them. Have not these lowly-born Sudras human souls in their bodies? Why do we resent the foreign rule while daily we torture the untouchables and treat them ten times worse than slaves? Ten times worse or twenty thousand times worse than serfs? Let those who do not believe in the essential wickedness of man come over to India and study the facts for themselves. The followers of Muhammad are ahead of the followers of Manu in this respect. We Musalmans have lost every sentiment of sympathy for the downtrodden people. We are as much responsible for keeping down the Sudras as Hindus, if not more. We also have our full share in killing human dignity and self-respect in them, and still we boast of professing Islam. What an appalling picture of hypocrisy the Musalman of India is. Against the behests of Islam, he takes pride in birth, and even upper classes of the Indian Musalman look down upon those who belong to the masses. They have formed an aristocracy of birth, but not of mind. They profess Islam, but follow Hinduism.

Sudras as a people are centuries deep in rot. Who will pull them to their feet, wipe their faces, and transform them? Once I expected great things from the noble-minded Mahatma Gandhi, but when he staked his all to deprive them of the right of a separate electorate, all hope was dashed to the ground. For one nationhood, a joint electorate is a necessity, but for those who are treated worse than dogs, a separate electorate is the only balm that can heal the [age-long] sore of untouchability. A separate electorate is the device to recognize the right of those who were so grossly wronged. Nothing less than the recognition of separate political rights can save them from the exploitation of their countrymen. They have had enough of our love; they must cultivate a spirit of hate against us Hindus and [Muslims] if they desire to live as human beings. They should not listen to our sweet sermons and good wishes. We have not an iota of sincerity left in us. Is there any place on the face of the earth where human beings are so contemptuously treated? Excepting a few people, Hindus and Musalmans as a whole are faithfully holding to their traditions. Musalman and Hindu leaders are actuated by political motives only in making friends with them.

Beware, for it is a snare and a delusion. You Sudras require your full social and political rights, but if you agree to be tied down to the wheel of Hindus and Musalmans, you will be doomed for another thousand years. Leaders of the untouchables should approach this serious problem in a spirit of realism. Never think that a microscopic minority of [Hindu and Muslim] Leaders will be able in the very near future to break through the formidable wall of orthodoxy. [Hindu and Muslim] masses are not going to budge an inch from their determined attitudes toward you. Leaders of the untouchables yielded under the threat of Mahatma Gandhi. To my mind, both sinned against scores of people who are suffering from the true old disgrace and humiliation.

The duty of the leaders of the untouchables and their sympathizers is plain. They must blow the breath of life in the nostrils of those downtrodden people by making them realize how their countrymen have treated them. In other words, unless you inculcate a spirit of hate in their minds against the [Hindu and Muslim] masses, they will never be able to stand on their feet. A separate electorate afforded them this opportunity. Now, under the scheme of joint electorates, no untouchable will raise his [or her] voice against the treatment meted out to them. They are again thrown on the mercy of those who have never shown any love for them. I am sure that Hindus and Muslims will curse my reasoning because they belong to the communities of the exploiters. Can temple entry movement and inclusion of one or two untouchables as ministers in the provincial cabinets change the phase of Indian life? It may be called a slight improvement, but it is not a change in the outlook of the people. At this slow pace, it will take another thousand years to complete the journey. Only a violent revolt against the existing social order can save the untouchables. Any fraternizing effort of League and Congress, Gandhis and Jinnahs will not master our time-honored habit of looking at untouchables as low people.

Any movement based on love cannot dispel pride from a human heart. Hate is the only known antidote to pride; pride is otherwise an incurable disease. People infected with natural and caste pride cannot be aroused to passionate action. Conscience does not plead the cause of those who are weak and exploited. Wolf is no fit shepherd and caste Hindus and Musalmans are exploiters; they should not be trusted with the uplift work. It is a mad belief that Mahatma Gandhi or Mr. Jinnah will transform the old Adam into a new man. The salvation of the untouchables lies in their own awakening based on the philosophy of hate for those who are responsible for their miseries. The philosophy of love, self-denying, and self-sacrifice is injurious in the case of those who have been dispossessed for so long, denied every human right, and sacrificed for the sons of the high houses and high castes.

What I prescribe for Sudras I cannot prescribe for a Muslim because he has already learned the virtue of retaliating too much, and he is in a position to hit back. Sometimes he is lured to take a mad plunge into destruction and chaos. But Sudras are lying prostrate, too weak to raise a hand in protest; hence, hate will give them the necessary strength. Those people who are now engaged in an apparently very plausible act of uplifting the Sudras are agents of the capitalist and high caste people. They only want to lull the untouchables into sleep.

An Ahrar friend, Moulana Abdul Qayyum of Cawnpore, who is also a convict in this jail, informs me that Hindu workers are preaching the philosophy of hate against the Musalmans among the untouchables, with the result that the untouchables now consider the Musalmans untouchables throughout Uttar Pradesh, Bihar, and Orissa. This state of affairs, if true, is a message of hope. Musalmans amply deserve this treatment. Let the Musalman be the first to suffer. Hindus will sooner or later suffer as sure as death the same fate at the hands of the Sudras. Let us at any cost instill the spirit of hatred in them to awaken them; then, the philosophy of love will transform them. But we must restore them to their consciousness by some injection so that they may feel the indignity hurled on them. If we do so, we will reform the Sudras and ourselves, [and] then love will reign in the country.

Chaudhry Afzal Haq
After his release from Rawalpindi Jail in
1941

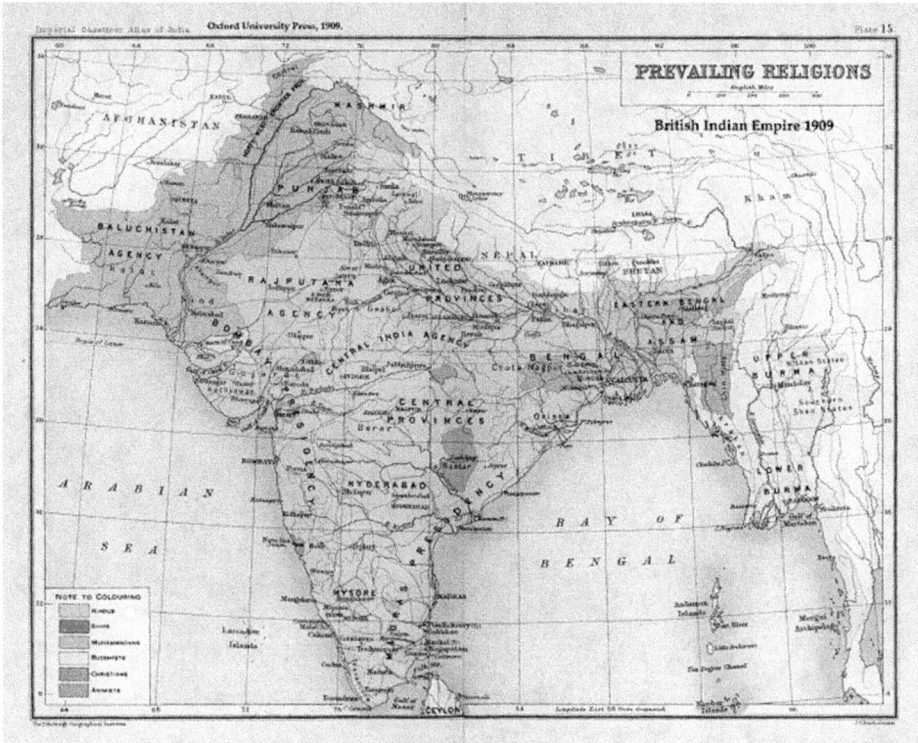

The map of the religions of British India during Afzal Haq's lifetime.

Source: Courtesy of Wikipedia

3

Economy

Muslims do not live within their means and never lay something by for a rainy day. Yes, that is the rule. The economic system of Islam does not permit individuals to put by anything for emergencies. Individualism is an unpardonable sin; you amass money at the expense of the poor; that is the economic formula of this religion. Usury is considered a cardinal crime. Islam, being a proletarian faith for a classless society, cannot encourage people to make their pile. Whoever owns any private property owns it on behalf of the state, and the state has full right to regulate property as it deems proper. There are certain restrictions against spending money at will. A person holding private property is not allowed to spend even a pie on luxury. Khalid, the greatest general of Islam, was asked why he gave away ten thousand rupees to a poet. It was held by Caliph Omar that Khalid had given this money either from the treasury or from his own pocket. In the former case, he had misappropriated, and in the latter case, he was extravagant. Therefore, he deserved dismissal on either count.

When Khalid submitted his case for revision, the Caliph further confiscated 20,000 rupees. It was not possible for Caliph Omar to let anyone who was a waster with such a large sum of money go only to be tempted again. The Prophet and his companions always looked upon wealth and private possessions as a great evil. Caliph Omar never hesitated to confiscate the property of those who were thought to be getting fat. This confiscated money did not go to the pockets of any individual; it was expended on the poor. There was ample common fund for common cause, and Muslim society flourished without wealthy individuals. A classless society can only flourish when there are other people living according to capitalistic rules of economy side by side with them. Jews and Christians lived with the Musalmans, but they were not allowed to give money to a Musalman on interest and thus upset the economic equilibrium of a classless society.

Here in India, the whole economic system of Islam received a setback. Fate ordained the Muslims to live with strange people who not only worshipped Lakshmi, the goddess of wealth, but also were used to treating human beings as impure and untouchable. The law of the land did not give any protection to Musalmans from the exploitation of the non-Muslims, while the precept of religion forbade them from exploiting others. The Muslims had to go to the wall as a result. Add to it the one-way flow of the country's wealth due to untouchability. A Hindu will not buy anything from a Muslim shop as far as possible. A Musalman is a permanent customer of the Hindu. Hindus have the sole monopoly of the Indian trade. There exist a few Muslim businessmen as an exception to prove the rule.

One will say that it is not due to untouchability that Musalmans lag behind in trade, but that their laziness of mind and extravagance are responsible for their present state of affairs. I recognize that both the factors are detrimental to the economic life of the Muslims (i.e., their own extravagance and the treatment by the Hindus). Englishmen, though nicknamed as a nation of shopkeepers, could not compete with a Hindu shopkeeper because of his very sporting habits. How can a nation of spendthrift habits like Musalmans live among such careful people as Hindus without losing it all someday? Englishmen, like Hindus, will patronize the British firm fist and will go to a Hindu and Muslim firm last. Musalmans did not create such prejudices in their minds with the result that they were obliged to make way for Hindus in the economic life of the country.

Very recently, with a little political and religious awakening, a section of the Musalmans has come to the conclusion that unless they develop the same prejudices as the Hindus have developed, they will not be able to stand on their feet. They incessantly preach the social boycott of Hindus just as the latter have boycotted them. Some of these preachers do realize that a change for the better is coming over Hindu society, but they maintain that this change is so slow that it will not be effective even after centuries, and Musalmans will grow weaker and weaker day by day. They have no faith in the reformative steps of the Congress. Muslim masses are ready to place their reliance on socialism, but they find little or no response to this movement in the Hindu society. In the new social order, Musalmans will hope to be treated as equals, but so long as the old order continues, their lot cannot change. Go to any Muslim shop and you will seldom see a Hindu customer, but Hindu shops are still full of Muslim customers. The "Buy Muslim" slogan is still weak because it is a movement uncontrolled and un-organized. But feelings against Hindus are always there.

A curious phenomenon — Muslims hate Hindus, and Hindus continue their hate-inspiring treatment; still, Musalmans flock to the Hindu shop. This shows that any boycott movement, unless skillfully organized and made a part of religion, is bound to fail. We experienced enough of it in the boycott movement of the Congress. Every Indian knew the disastrous effect of the foreign-made articles on the national economy and easily took the pledge to "Buy Indian" when the boycott movement was at its zenith. After some months, enthusiasm cooled down, and in spite of genuine feeling, people again began to buy foreign goods. In spite of great resentment against the treatment by Hindus, Muslim customers still flock to Hindu shops in any number.

I mention that Hindus do not shun the Muslim shops because of spite, but because it is their habit of life not to visit a Muslim shop. Since I do not buy sweetmeats, milk, bread, and the like from those Hindus who treat me as untouchable, it has become my habit not to buy anything from a Hindu shop. I do not hate any Hindu; still, my steps seldom turn toward a Hindu shop. Though the Hindus like to treat Muslims as untouchables only so far as the cooked articles are concerned, they have now developed a subconscious mindset that leads them only to the Hindu shops. If they go to a Muslim shop, they go there with an effort. Here lies the secret of economic ruin of the Muslim community. I am at one with those who say that Musalmans earn with difficulty, spend with less care, and have a natural dislike for keeping account. But their incompetence in money matters combined with the prohibition against usury is not sufficient to put them at the mercy of moneylenders.

The stigma of their being untouchable goes a long way in destroying businesses in which he, a Muslim, invests money, because he cannot command the patronage of the Hindu public. It is not a fancy but a fact that 70 percent of Musalmans still go to a Hindu shop, and only 5 percent of the Hindus patronize any Muslim. Muslims, as a community, are hard pressed and have been going through deep waters for some decades. Hindus make it a point that no Musalman may be able to get any shop in a Hindu bazaar. At first, Hindus and Musalmans were living in different quarters, and in order to make themselves safer, the Hindus erected big doors with iron bars where a Muslim hawker could not gain admittance. I would add insult to injury if I asked any untouchable, "Why do you not do any business? ". No Hindu, [and] no Muslim, will go to patronize him, and members of his own community have not yet acquired the communal spirit sufficient to "buy from the untouchables". Therefore, there is no hope of untouchables buying from untouchables only. Hence, there is not an iota of a chance for an untouchable to flourish as a trader.

The case of the [Muslims] comes next to the untouchables. Hindus [also] consider Muslims as untouchables; therefore, Muslims have little chance of success in any business. This is why it is generally felt by shrewd Muslims that unless Muslims develop the same prejudices as the Hindus have done, their future in India is gloomy. Pulpits of the Musalmans do not help them because Islam prohibits its followers from considering any body as impure and untouchable. Mosques are the only fit places to carry on such propaganda, but a Mullah finds himself helpless in this respect. Muslim theologians have not considered this question as a body. So the "Buy Muslim" movement is only a mass movement in the sense that masses feel the pinch of the Hindu treatment, but there is no leader to put any constructive program before them in order that they may be saved from the daily humiliation. Any aggrieved community that finds no peaceful way to give vent to its feelings generally resorts to violence. Music before the mosques and taking out processions of cows meant to be slaughtered on Eid Day is nothing but the eruption of pent-up feelings.

If you go diligently through the history of communal troubles and its causes, you will come to the same conclusions as I have.

The Muslim masses before the advent of the British Raj were inert, and the classes being the governing class had their own pride and sense of superiority over the Hindus. So there was no communal feeling in the community; hence, there was no trouble. Englishmen are considered by Hindu masses as untouchable as Musalmans. But no Englishman has any ill feeling against Hindus, because Hindus of High Houses who go to them do not dare to put them to humiliation. They dine with them and invite them to their tables. But when the present order will collapse and when Englishmen have to live here as Indians, not as rulers, they would then feel the pinch of untouchability.

Muslim ruling classes did not feel it in Mughal times. Even today, they do not feel it to the full because the capitalist class among the Hindus does not properly observe the rules of Hindu society, but Muslim classes now have only begun to appreciate the plight of the Muslim masses on account of Hindu untouchability. British officers felt the need of studying the question of present debt, and they prominently brought to light the growing poverty of Muslim masses and in their own novel way tried to help them. They did not bring the untouchability question into prominence through fear of the Hindus. The English Government wanted to drag the Sudras out of the clutches of the Hindus, but Mahatma Gandhi threatened to fast unto death. The government, fearing the political consequences of it, let down the Sudras. Untouchability is the worst form of slavery. All credit is due to the High soul of Mannu, who has left the sons of the soil to live not as separate nations, but as enemies engaged in an unending war. Today when I was writing this, I received the *Daily Tribune* for 27 May 1940, which contained a very recent article by Mahatma Gandhi published in the *Harijan*. I give it below in order to show that what I have written is not an exaggerated view of the situation:

[Bombay, May 25]

I have no hesitation whatsoever in saying that he who has the slightest untouchability in him is wholly unfit for enrollment in the Satyagraha Sana. I regard untouchability as the root cause of our downfall and Hindu-Muslim discord. Untouchability is the curse of Hinduism and therefore of India. The taint is so pervasive that it haunts man even after he has changed over to another faith.

Mahatma Gandhi writes in today's [*Harijan*] in answer to a correspondent's question as to whether Gandhiji agrees that it ought to be made an absolute rule in the Satyagarh camps that no one who regards the touch of harijans [Shudra's]as polluting and does not freely mix with them should be permitted to attend them.

Replying to another question, it does not prove (to be) a short-cut to the removal of untouchability if the Congress started a plan to train harijans as expert cooks for Hindu homes and made it a rule to man every ashram or mess meant for the Congress with harijan cooks thus trained[?]. Gandhiji writes,

Our ambition should be to enable the harijan to rise to the highest rank, but while that must be the ideal, it would be a good thing to train some harijans to become accomplished cooks. I have observed that the more we draw them into the domestic service the quicker is the pace of reform. Harijans who become absorbed in our homes lose all sense of inferiority and become a living link between other harijans and Savama Hindus.

United Press [writes]

"It is a matter of great satisfaction that the great leader of India has come to the right conclusion at last. But nothing has yet been done to show that Congress leaders will take up the matter earnestly. Mahatma Gandhi devotes his whole time and energy to removing the taint of untouchability from the Sudras, but makes a passing reference to the treatment of the Musalmans by the Hindus, which shows to an ordinary man that Mahatamaji has no heart to remove the stigma of untouchability from the Muhammadans, whereas the Muhammadans deserve the same amount of attention as the Sudras."

Mahatma must know that an attempt is being made to embrace the Sudras to use them against Musalmans. Musalmans have no right to blame the Hindu leader of nationalist India because he is surrounded by those luminaries who are more interested in Sudras than Muslims, and Musalmans have made no serious attempt to deserve his attention. Some Muslims call Mahatamaji a shrewd little bania who has only sweet words for

Musalmans and in his heart of hearts likes to see Muslims as underdogs of Hindus. This is a malicious construction on the working of Mahatma's mind.

We Musalmans never put our social problems to him, never sought his advice, and in fact never patiently heard him. He is, after all, a human being capable of being influenced by the environment. As long as big brothers Moulana Muhammad Ali and Shoukat Ali were with Gandhiji, he was thinking more in terms of a Musalman than of a Hindu. The fates ordained otherwise. The Mahatma, who was in the pocket of the Ali Brothers, has been thrown into the laps of those who naturally think in terms of a Hindu. Moulana Azad is a scholar. Scholars are always shy and incapable of influencing the character of those with whom they come in touch. They think it below their dignity to talk freely with anybody and [to] assert their point of view. So, Musalmans are out of court so far as the Mahatma is concerned. Moreover, the efforts of one man, however great, cannot be crowned with success when the problem to be tackled is so puzzling. Hindu society is always desirous of excluding others. Reform in such an essentially exclusive society is not an easy matter. Here in the Punjab, there is a national institution called the Servants of the People Society controlled by first-class Hindu patriots of the province. Firstly, they never admitted any Musalman into that society, because as a people, Hindus are brought up in an exclusive atmosphere, and they feel a certain amount of uneasiness among Muslim society. Secondly, the donors are Hindus, and if they dare to admit any Muhammadans, they will lose the sympathy of Hindu philanthropists. There is an insurance company managed by highly patriotic people, but they seldom employ a Muhammadan. So, mere verbal generosity of outlook cannot solve the practical difficulties. Moreover, if Gandhiji does not realize this and someone presses upon him the desirability of propagating against the exclusiveness of Hindus in the economic field, do you think any Hindu will hear him? No, this is expecting too much of them.

In short, Hindus do not only shut out Musalmans from social circles, but also do not admit them in business. On the contrary, banias in a Muhammadan village are still living like lords wielding authority and having prestige, but in the villages of Hindu Jats, they are looked down upon, and in the villages of Sikhs, they are harassed. Muhammadans were never considered fit for benevolent treatment even at the hands of banias. This exclusiveness of the Hindu in the field of economics has made the position of the Musalman very pitiable and has left no potentiality in the rank and file to work out a constructive program. Now Muslim masses have become very touchy on account of poverty and can be easily excited to fly at a Hindu's throat. They have had to pay very dearly for their madness. They kill Hindus but are hanged proportionately in larger numbers and bring calamity to a still greater number of their dependents.

I invite your attention to a very recent public appeal made by the secretary of the Muslim League Sindh with regard to the pressing need of monetary help for those who are arrested in connection with (Manzilgah) Sukkar riots. Sayyed Ali Mohammad Secretary says,

There are altogether 1,800 Musalmans who are being prosecuted in different cases. Those who are shut in the four walls of jail have left behind them starving families, women, and children, and have no clothes to wear. Up to this time, several Muhammadans have been given capital sentences and some others were given long-term imprisonment. I appeal to all Musalmans in the name of those starving women and children to send as much help as they can.

As a visitor of the Punjab jails, I was informed of many cases of the Muslim rioters with very long sentences whose women and children were starving, and there was none to look after them. The Muslim masses are poverty stricken and unorganized. Classes are careless and callous. In spite of all those miseries, the Muslim masses will continue to be furious and riotous because they are treated as aliens in their own country. Our first need is that Hindus should take upon themselves the duty of forming a strong organization to combat those who consider Musalmans as untouchables. If a Muhammadan organization will take up this duty, it will further embitter the feelings.

In the year 1925, Majlas-i-Ahrar workers formed the Punjab Khilafat Committee and took to preaching against the treatment of Hindus. Hindus resented such preaching. The government threatened to take action against those who were in any way connected with this agitation. This taint of untouchability is to be removed somehow or other from the Muslims. If Hindus condemn their co-religionists, it will pave the way to Hindu-Muslim unity, and if any Muslim organization will take up this agitation, Hindus will resent such an attitude on the part of the Muslims.

When Seva Samti was formed, Muhammadans were very glad that this organization would help the Musalman in raising their voices against their treatment by Hindus. But to their utter dismay and disappointment, this organization devised new instruments of humiliating Musalmans. Seva Samti volunteers offered water in glasses to Hindus, and for thirsty Musalmans and scavenges, they used a hollow bamboo pipe. They would pour in water at one end, and it came out from the other end of the pipe. By this contrivance, Hindu volunteers were saved from the polluting touch of the Musalmans and Sudras. They gave water and took away self-respect. This service resulted in more hatred. In spite of bamboo being a nonconductor, if the hand of an impure Musalman touched the pipe in the course of gulping down water, he was taken to task. Such pipes were generally used for pouring down country medicines in the throats of cows and buffaloes in our villages.

Forty years ago, no Muslim was employed as a waterman at a railway station throughout India. Even the Muslims of high houses were humiliated by Hindu watermen. Muhammadans have now pressed upon the railway authorities the desirability of making separate water arrangements for Musalmans. Hindu water and Muslim water is echoed at every station at the arrival and departure of every train. This is a standing contradiction of the one nation theory. If there is any true nationalist among the Hindus, it is his duty to encourage all silent voices among the Musalmans whose brains are not yet deadened and who loathe the treatment by Hindus. If Hindus encourage Musalmans, there will be peace and goodwill reigning in the country. If Muhammadans are left to themselves to remedy the state of affairs, there will be chaos and confusion in India.

Everybody will admit that the present state of affairs should not be long allowed to continue. Some Hindu organization should come forward with the sole object of preaching for better social treatment of the Musalmans. On account of humiliating social treatment by Hindus, I see Musalmans journeying into a new life. This would be the end of our political aspirations. Muhammadans are very hard-pressed by the social and economic boycott of the Hindus, and they are going through deep waters today. As a countermove, they are developing the boycott spirit in them. Though it is no easy matter to boycott those who are financially better, and though this task is beset with difficulties, they have become desperate. They are already left to fry in summer and freeze in winter, and the social treatment by their Hindu countrymen is still very exasperating.

Gifted orators like Atta Ullah Shah could not rouse Muslims to patriotic action because they see that in spite of the fact that the same mother India bears and nourishes them, they are considered untouchables by those who expect them to shed their blood for the common cause. So, a Muslim thinks that his home is the earth and the world is his fatherland, political problems of India are outside his sphere, and he has no right to approach them in the light of one nationhood until the social and economic tangles are straightened out.

4

Language

A common language is the first ingredient of a nation. In this respect, we are very unfortunate. There are dozens of language groups in this country. Hindus and Muslims break each other's heads over the rival claims of Hindi and Urdu. Our spoken language in Upper India is Hindustani, which is understandable by every inhabitant of that part of the country, but the written languages are Persianized Urdu and Sanskritized Hindi. A great battle is raging around this question, which tends to widen the gulf between the two communities more and more. The beauty of a language consists in spoken and written languages being one and the same, but the hysterical attempt to make Hindustani look like Persian or Sanskrit is making the question of language rather a difficult affair.

Urdu, as its name indicates, was the honest attempt on the part of both Hindus and Muhammadans to evolve a common language for the whole people of this country. Urdu assimilated all the appropriate words of Sanskrit, Persian, Punjabi, Arabic, and English. As this communal struggle went on unabated, the Hindus naturally wanted Hindi to be made the medium of instruction. In the Moghul period, Persian was the court language. In the British Raj, Persian yielded its place to the English and Urdu languages. Musalmans still think that they evolved Urdu as a common language and that the Hindus' claim about Hindi is only a spoke in the wheel. Hindus feel that it is their natural right to popularize *Hindi*. So they [clash] with each other and are ready to break each other's necks. Sometimes before the partition of Bengal, the Bihar Government raised the question of Urdu and Hindi. The action of the Bihar Government preyed on the minds of Musalmans. After the partition of Bengal, agitation in favor of Punjabi was started in the Punjab as a medium of instruction. Hindus took interest against Urdu, and from their attitude, Muslims concluded that they were paying off old scores. The Muslims laid great stress on the adoption of Urdu as a *lingua franca* for the whole country; the more they stressed, the more the Hindus resented, and in a few years' time, Hindus discarded Urdu and began to popularize Hindi with a vengeance.

Hindus with comparatively vast financial resources enriched the Hindi literature within a few years. In the natural course of events though, Urdu is still the popularly spoken language, Hindi as the written language has stolen a march over Urdu, and Urdu is now lagging behind Hindi because of Hindu capitalists and politicians. Congress governments and the film industry have given impetus to it. Muhammadans who follow the policy of "spend and God will send" are left to mourn like a poor passenger who cannot afford to buy a ticket for an outgoing train and sets out on foot to reach the destination.

Young Muslim authors who express themselves in Urdu do not lack the qualities of head and heart, but they cannot make a living and are soon fed up with this thankless task. Munshi [Prem] Chand, a great storywriter, is an outstanding example of this. He began his stories in Urdu. In spite of being highly popular, he could not manage to make both ends meet. But when he began to write in Hindi, he was well off after a few years. The most popular book in Urdu is purchased in hundreds only, but in Hindi a book is purchased in thousands because the Hindu public can afford to do so, and Musalmans generally borrow books or make use of the libraries. A poverty-stricken community, however gay, cannot produce good literature, because it is the result of long and patient study of a subject, and that cannot be pursued without encouragement and patronage. There are so many Urdu writers. Every subject they touch turns to a story under their hands, but poverty reduces them to skeletons on account of their fault of being Urdu writers.

It is hysterical to attempt to thrust Urdu on Hindu citizens. They are not favorably inclined toward it. They have every right to preserve the language they love. Poor people always have poor literature; rich people cannot be made to cast off their own rich literature. There are certain Muslims who accept the two-nation theory and still expect Hindus to adopt the Urdu language. Congressional attempts to make Hindustani the *lingua franca* should be welcomed by Musalmans, but it must be clearly understood that this Hindustani must naturally be Sanskritized Hindustani. Muhammadans are no doubt lovers of high literature, but on economic and political grounds, they cannot make Urdu a popular language. I know that Hindu politicians from the core of their hearts wish to settle the language question once and for all, but it is a very intricate question and cannot be settled in a decade.

Too much insistence upon Urdu is an outcome of a social disease. Muhammadans and Hindus both live in watertight compartments. Therefore, they cannot be expected to evolve a common language satisfactorily unless and until their social relations are much improved. Urdu was built on the ruins of Persian and Arabic, with Indian national and united Hindu-Muslim efforts. But very soon, it became the language of the untouchables and unworthy of Hindu use. Hence, any attempt to make Urdu a *lingua franca* would be futile. Hindi is also the language of Kafir, and a believer would not learn it. Every Hindu and Musalman should try to know both scripts, Hindi and Urdu. This does not mean that we will be able to evolve a common language soon. Continuous suggestions by marching and drilling, leads a regiment to a rigid uniformity of action; common language leads to a rigid uniformity of a nation in its thinking. But this uniformity of thought and action is essentially based on social and political unity, which is absent in the case of India.

A German who reads the French language does not begin to think as a Frenchman because their politics are different. We Hindus and Musalmans not only have our respective different historic backgrounds, even socially we consider each other untouchables. So every rule becomes an exception in our case, and the situation becomes puzzling. Our social prejudices not only make our politics complicated, but they also make our whole lives a hell and make the question of a *lingua franca* for the whole of India a knotty problem. No one is ready to give way; therefore, no satisfactory solution is possible. Every attempt to evolve a common language will be met with opposition, because we are living as enemies. Those who wish well of the country and want peace can only help this cause by learning both scripts. In my weak condition of health and old age, I have now learned to read the Hindi Primary Readers. Though I like the Urdu language very much, a peep into Hindi is delightful.

There is another complication—that of provincial languages. Though Punjabi is not understood even in the whole of the province, its claim to be the medium of instruction is put forward by the Sikh Community. Urdu is, in fact, polished Punjabi, but Sikhs are not contented with Urdu. They do not even like Hindi. They have evolved a script of their own out of Hindi. So there are not only dialects of one language, but languages within language in this country. One language could be a factor in keeping all of the people of India together, but our responsible leaders fall out on this question daily. All honest attempts of the Congress leaders have been foiled in solving the question of the language. Unless the malady of untouchability is removed and people begin to live like brothers, they will not be able to evolve a common language.

Hindu masses are very tough in all things that give them superiority over the Muslim masses. When there is a section of Hindu politicians who are eager to see Hindus and Muslims living as brothers, there is another section that works day and night for the continuance of the old order. I had an occasion to visit the office of a Hindu trust. While sitting and waiting for the manager, I saw a library adjacent to the office where some gentlemen were reading newspapers and some others were taking notes from certain books. Instead of waiting outside, I thought it fit to read some papers in the library. No sooner did I enter the room than all eyes were turned on me. They looked astonished and perplexed. Almost all of them who were reading or writing ceased to do their work and began to look at my face and the faces of one another. It at once flashed across my mind that I was not wanted there, but why? Suddenly, I saw on boards hanging on every wall with inscriptions in bold letters: FOR HINDUS ONLY. I am told that it was the life mission of the Hindu philanthropist to keep the superiority complex of Hindus intact. This trust is perhaps the biggest in India. With such exclusive training of the mind still going on, no one can hope to solve the language question overnight. Let us wait and see how almighty God orders our destiny after this world war.

5

Politics

Hindus are socially intolerant, but politically their leaders are farsighted and broadminded. They are a little hesitant no doubt, but not incorrigible and unprogressive. They will give a patient hearing to every proposal and will try to find a way out of the difficulty. Politically, they are quite sincere and try their level best to act as nationalists. They only deviate under the great pressure of their masses; otherwise, in the natural course of things, they are prepared to go to great lengths to oblige the Muslim community. There would have been more breaking of heads than hitherto, but the sufferings endured by these Hindus for the country's cause have melted the hearts of even those Musalmans who have their natural abhorrence of Hindus because of their unbearable social treatment. These Hindu leaders attracted the noblest among the Muslims. The flower of the Hindu and Muslim communities in the Congress organization [has] suffered much in [it's] attempt to blend the two peoples into one nation. But their efforts have not so far been crowned with success. Why? Because, they did not proceed with the country's problem scientifically.

The Lucknow Pact of 1916 is a proof, if any proof is needed, of the fact that Hindu leaders on their own accord conceded separate electorates and thus bridged the gulf that had been created by laying the foundation of the Muslim League. This move on the part of Hindu leaders brought Hindus and Muslims of the upper classes closer to each other. Though Hindus and Muslims are still a separate people, the government feared that they could sit together and speak with one voice. It added to the prestige of the country.

Hindus of the Mahasabha mentality believe that separate electorates are the root cause of the present strife, but even before that attempt, we were living as alien people always ready to fly at each other's throats. We have yet to produce that resourceful man who will be able to fuse various prejudices into one creative drive. Politics is the art of doing what is possible under the circumstances to the best of one's ability. I recognize the nobility of soul of the Congress leaders who never gave way to despair and always doggedly tried to find ways and means to adjust all quarrels.

As a natural corollary to the new reforms, Muhammadans wanted to make up the deficiency in different services, but it was resented by the Hindu educated community, who held the sole monopoly of some of the services. Since the year 1922, every government office became the propaganda center for broadcasting the message of hate. The Hindu and Muslim press bitterly attacked each other. There were riots and breaking of heads. Hindus and Musalmans who had come nearer to embracing each other began once more to take leave of each other as if for forever. The Congress leadership was alarmed. Mr. Das, the great leader of Bengal, notified his intention to allot 60 percent of the public services in those districts and Municipal Boards where Muhammadans formed a majority. He actually raised the percentage of Musalmans in the Calcutta Corporation.

The Maha Sahba leaders raised a storm of protest against him, but he steered his ship through this storm until his valuable life was cut short by heart trouble. Together with other Hindu leaders, Mr. Sirinavasa Iyenger, President of the Congress in 1926, thought that the cause of the Hindu-Muslim trouble was political. Hence, he wanted to know what Muslim demands might be in the case of Puraa swaraj. Muslim leaders, including the late Moulana Mohd Ali and Mr. Jinnah, met in Delhi and formulated very moderate proposals to be included in the Hindu-Muslim pact. They demanded reservations of seats according to population based on joint electorates. It is curious that even this proportion did not find favor with some of the Hindu Sabha leaders, and consideration of it was postponed. A unity conference was called a year later to further discuss the matter.

At a number of these conferences, I saw that Mr. Muhammad Ali Jinnah tried his level best to come to an agreement with Hindus, but his efforts were not crowned with success because of a Hindu gentleman of renown who was afterward taken as a member of the Congress working committee. Mr. Jinnah, from the very beginning of his political career, was a staunch supporter of joint electorates and a great advocate of the one-nation theory. But that Hindu gentleman left no stone unturned to exasperate Mr. Jinnah in the unity conferences.

The Muslim League was split into two parts. One section led by Mr. Jinnah and supported by the late Moulana Mohd Ali, Shoukat Ali, Dr. Ansari, and other nationalist leaders held Muslim League sessions in Calcutta, and the other section led by Mian Sir Fazi-i-Hussain and Mian Sir Shati held their session in Lahore. The former had the good wishes of the Hindu leaders, and the latter had the backing of the British Government. One advocated joint electorates, and the other demanded rights on the basis of separate electorates. Congressional leaders were very anxious to offer a common front against British imperialism. So, in their anxiety to do so, they called an all-party conference to be held in Lucknow to consider a new pact on the basis of the Nehru Report.

Muhammadan politicians were anxious to secure the support of Hindus for the separation of Sind from Bombay Presidency. Hindu Sabha leaders opposed the proposal tooth and nail, but the Congress spokesmen of Sind brought strange facts to light, which goes to show that our political policies change with the wind. A Hindu congressman informed the conference that a few years ago, the Hindu communalists demanded the separation of Sind from Bombay Presidency, and Muslim communalists opposed this proposal. But now the position is reversed. This is how prejudice works. Congressional leaders were satisfied that there was no fundamental difference between the claims of the different communities. The Nehru Report tried its best to dissipate the fear from the hearts of the Musalmans.

The case of the Punjab always presented a difficulty because of the fact that there is triangular counter-strife. The Hindus and Sikhs want a greater share than is justified by their strength in services, Municipal Boards, and Legislative Assembly, and the Muslims want to retain their bare majority. Hence, an adjustment becomes impossible. In the conference, every province was eager to adjust its differences in the best spirit, but the Punjab was making a very poor show of its talents and tolerance. At last in a sub-committee that was attended by Sir Tej Bahadur Sapru, P. Mori Lal, Pandit Madan, Mohan Malvi Moulana Azad, Sarojani Naidu, Lala Lajpat Rai, and others, warring elements of the Punjab were made to accept joint electorates. The Sikhs were the first to declare their acceptance. Muhammadans acceded willy-nilly to the wishes of the leaders. However, the Congress, khilafat, and Akali workers signed the Punjab Pact.

But to our astonishment, that very day the Sikhs began to show their misgivings; the next day they mildly protested, and the day after, they clamored against the pact. It added more to our astonishment when we saw the whole Hindu press supporting the Sikhs. The Sikhs always allowed themselves to be used as pawns in all political games of the Hindu communalists, and even some Congress Hindus have a soft heart for Sikhs. Both Mahatamaji and Pandit Malviaji supported the Sikhs in their protest against the Punjab Pact. Sikhs now demanded that their seats should be fixed according to population and that they should be further allowed to contest any number of seats in the Punjab under the scheme of joint electorates.

Muhammadans already had a bare majority in the province; they could not be a party to this arrangement. Moreover, joint electorates were never favored by the Muslim masses. Those who signed the Punjab Pact among the Muslims became the target, and Muslim Communalists attacked them fiercely. Khilafat workers who were the signatories of the pact were in very deep waters in those days. But they continued propaganda in favor of the original Punjab Pact. But Congress withdrew the Nehru Report, and the Punjab Pact *ipso facto* went with it. This must be noted that Mr. Jinnah, favoring the joint electorates, wanted some minor changes in the Nehru Report, but Mahatamaji did not yield.

However, after the Nehru Report had been thrown in the river, Ravi Khilafatist Musalmans continued to favor joint electorates, but it was unimagined even by the most imaginative among them that Dr. Ansari in his Faridpore speech would make overtures to the Sikhs on the basis of their new claim. But the

Muslim nationalist workers did not find their backs equal to this burden, and they gave way, forming a new organization called Majlis-i-Ahrar. Hindu leaders did not lose heart and continued their search for a common formula satisfactory to all. Mahatma Gandhi joined the Round Table Conference, and Muslims were ready to accept the joint electorates, but the Sikhs confused the issue by making extravagant claims. Mahatma Gandhi, as the sole representative of the Congress, could not take his courage in both his hands and rebuke the Sikhs for their immoderate demands.

Mr. Ramsay Macdonald was asked to give an award on the claims of the different communities. Unfortunately, the award of the Premier was a bolt from the blue for non-Muslim politicians, and the Sikhs threatened bloodshed. Another unity conference was called, but it also ended in smoke. It may again be noted that Mr. Jinnah was dropped out of the picture in the Second Round Table Conference because he was a staunch supporter of one nationhood and an advocate of joint electorates. Mian Sir Fazi-i-Hussain was a shrewd politician; newsmongers said that he was responsible for the great mischief done to the country's cause. He was a moderate leader, therefore a practical man. To communities and people, he used to say, "Seldom relinquish the advantage over other communities and people; hence, there is the necessity of hard fighting for our rights in this country."

After the communal award, he was quite satisfied. Now, he was anxious to come to terms with Hindus and Sikhs on the basis of joint electorates. He and Sir Joginder Singh agreed to a formula based on joint electorates, but both Sikh and Hindu leaders turned it down. When we accepted the Punjab Pact on the basis of joint electorates, he said that our scheme of joint electorates was not disastrous for Muslims, but he feared that Hindus and Sikhs could oppose us tooth and nail. Perhaps, knowing this weakness of the Hindus and Sikhs of the Punjab, he himself evolved a formula based on joint electorates to be finally rejected. He was sure as the sun in the heavens that Punjabi Hindus and Sikhs feared that they would be worse off under the scheme of joint electorates and therefore were not going to accept it easily.

However, Muhammadans under the communal award were given more than they expected, and Mian Fazal-i-Hussain was in a position to show magnanimity toward other communities, though only outwardly. Multan jail barracks were full of provincial and district office bearers of the Congress and Ahrar, when one morning the news of the award was brought in. Muhammadans were jubilant, and Hindus felt blue. Outside, the Sikhs threatened bloodshed in the province and took oaths before Guru Granth Sahib to revolt against the communal award. But Congress High Command kept its head and did not try to disturb the communal peace.

Congress accepted the award as the last resort because there was no way out of it. Congress accepted the ministries under the award, and the long-headed Congress Governments did their level best to hold the scales of justice even in trying circumstances. Human agencies are not without fault, but the defects of the Congress ministries were allowed to obscure their good features. At one time, the League spokesmen and press made much of the police firings on Khaksars in the United Provinces. Even a reasonable person among the Muslim Community pulled a very long face because of this incident, and the League MLAs set their face against Pandit Pan, the United Provinces premier. The Muslim masses were made to believe that, by suppression of the Khaksars, the Congress wanted to break the spirit of resistance in the Muslim Community. Khaksar day was celebrated. Muslim papers brought out "Khaksar Numbers." Now, Sir Sikandar's government in this province is obliged to do the same thing with a vengeance. Firings and prosecutions are of daily occurrence. The League is patiently looking at the bloody drama. No one can now dare say that the Unionist Government with a Muslim League at its head is breaking the backbone of the Community. The protest of the Muslim press, if it ever protests at all, sounds like an appeal that falls on deaf ears. You will tremble at the thought of the state of affairs if a similar Khaksar massacre had taken place anywhere under a Congress Government. Khaksars had a good time in United Provinces jails. They were treated as if they were state prisoners. But now in the Punjab Jails, they are being treated as ordinary criminals, and batches of them are tendering apologies.

In spite of the Communal award, League Leaders now claim the partition of India into two parts. They are dead sure of the support of the Muslim masses in any extravagant claim. The Muslim masses will be ever ready to pay with their lives, because as neighbors they are not satisfied with Hindu dealings. As a moneylender, he treats his Muslim client harshly, and as a countryman, he considers him impure. Hence, the Muslim masses want perpetual strife with Hindus. They cannot appreciate the generous move on the part of the Congress leaders. They look through colored spectacles on every move of the Hindu politicians, because in daily life they do not find an iota of generosity in any Hindu. Yet, they want revenge for the day-to-day treatment. They look upon him as their savior who goads them to continue the strife, and they look down upon the prince of peace as a traitor to the cause of the Community. "Toward animals in distress," they say, "Hindus are willing to extend their helping hand, but for human beings in distress, if he is a Muhammadan, they have little pity."

Treating the Muslims as impure and unclean is becoming unbearable day by day. Once a people begin to feel the indignity and insult, they can be goaded by clever people into any fanatical act. There lies the secret of a communalist's success and failure of those who preach Hindu-Muslim unity. The voices that were silent before are now encouraged. Muslims are now learning the art of speaking as they feel it. One of the ultra-nationalist Muslim workers confined in this jail said that enemies within the gates are not so badly treated as Musalmans in this country. Here are some German aliens confined in this jail; our Superintendent, a British Military Officer, has no hesitation in dining with them. But we people who live in a country and are a subject race treat each other worse than enemies. This state of affairs ought to set every congressman to thinking.

But the Congress program is naïve, if not primitive. They formed mass contact committees—lifeless bodies. They defeated their end very soon because Hindus fear Muslim contact, and the Congress is mum on this subject and does not try to expel prejudices from the Hindu mind. Congress has the Achut Udhar program, but it has no reference to the treatment of the Musalman. At least I have not heard any congressman condemning Hindus for their treatment of Musalmans. This four-anna membership is no contact with the Muslim masses. If Hindu members of the Congress are ordered by Gandhiji to dine with Musalmans, I am sure 95 percent of them will leave Congress. What do they mean by [Hindu-Muslim mass-contact] when the very touch of a Muslim Congressman makes his brother Hindu congressman unclean? Mass contact looks like hypocrisy, a mere deceit, and a fraud.

A young Hindu friend who is serving his term with us told me of his experience, which points to a moral. He, with other Congress workers, went to the villages to enroll members and address meetings. Muhammadans as usual gave the cold shoulder to them. Feeling thirsty, he entered a Muslim house, where an old lady was sitting. She asked him who he was. He replied that he was a Brahman. "Hindus never use anything touched by Muslims," she said. "Mother, I am not one of those; I stand for unity," he said. "You will succeed in your mission; those who treat Muslims as untouchables cannot," said I.

Every Hindu patriot who wishes well of the country should study this subject himself. I assure them all that when Muslim masses see a Muslim nationalist fighting shoulder to shoulder with a Hindu nationalist, they will at once jump to the conclusion that this man betrayed Islam for a mess of pottage for himself.

Hindus stand arraigned before the tribunal of history and humanity for treading upon the necks of their own countrymen. The polluting power of a dog and a lizard is not as great as that of a Musalman and a Sudra. Some Hindus, I am glad to say, are paying some attention toward the uplift of the untouchables other than Musalmans, because Mahasabha politicians want numerical preponderance to fight constitutional battles, and if need be, to arrange them against Musalmans. But without a change of heart, they will not be helpful to Sudras and will never be immune from danger.

Caste prejudices are the outcome of blind stupidity, incapable of recognizing the dignity of humanity. Once it is recognized, India will become the heaven of peace. Will Congress politicians muster sufficient courage to fight on the side of Musalmans in eradicating the evil of untouchability? Sometimes I fall prey to misgivings even about Congress friends when I see them crying hoarsely against the treatment of Sudras and never speaking a word against the treatment the Hindus meted out to Musalmans. Are they not inwardly feeling proud of this treatment? Do they not want to continue this state of affairs?

I console myself with the idea that the political awakening of Muslims will come to their help. Then, what about the theory of one nationhood in India? One nationhood is a stunt of a few politicians; it has no significance so far as Hindus and Muslims are concerned. Some say that a race is springing up that will soon revolutionize the mentality of the people and blend them into one nation. I say amen to it, but I am not very optimistic. New times will not come soon. Age long disease cannot be eradicated in a decade or two. There are still people in the Congress fold who justify untouchability. They say it is hygienic. I have seen some prominent men connected with the Congress holding the glass of water high in the air and turning their faces to the sky. They stand with open mouths, pouring water into their mouths, and gulping it down their throats in a very artistic way. Yes, it is hygienic, they say. It is maniacal, I say. Judge for yourself who is right.

I have been with Malviaji in Delhi Jail. He was a kind and considerate, but awfully tough, Brahman. What to speak of a Musalman who would not like to see even the shadow of a Hindu in his dining place? President Patel was a very jolly fellow. He knew the weakness of Pandatji and was used to visiting him just at the time of his meals. Patel used to stand before the sun in such a position that his shadow was cast on Malviaji. This otherwise sane Brahman would jump out of the choke like an enraged child. "What is the matter, Pandatji?" President Patel would ask.

How suffocating is the atmosphere of the Hindu society for a Musalman? No Hindu can dream of it. Unless we lay low the demon of untouchability, India, the paradise on earth, will continue to be a hell on account of communal strife. We must cease employing the language of hypocrisy and frankly admit that so long as untouchability lives, Hindus and Muslims cannot cultivate any social ties. I know that an attempt is being made to make chattels of the Musalmans and uplift the Sudras only, and then dominate India. Unfortunately, some Hindus have reached that stage in emotional stress when logical arguments cease to sway decisions, but I am sure that better sense will prevail some day in the country, though that day seems very remote.

I, as a Musalman, gratefully appreciate the enthusiasm of Congress politicians to come to an understanding with the Muslims. But no political move will be crowned with success unless the social ban is lifted from the Muhammadans. As I have already stated, Muslims feel the pinch of untouchability and social boycott by the Hindus very badly. The Muslims will embrace every opportunity to pick a quarrel with the Hindus, because life is not after their heart on account of the treatment meted out to them. Mr. Jinnah is the apple of their eyes so long as he promises to fight against those who have kept them down. No sooner will he come to terms with Hindus than he will be decried as a traitor.

The secret of leadership of the Muslim masses lies in goading them to constant strife with Hindus. A life of poverty and ill-treatment at the hands of the Hindus has made them desperate. They want to answer back injury for insult. Who does not know that poverty and ill-treatment belittle the mind and corrupt the spirit? Muhammadans think that Hindus are responsible for their woes. This is why they one day cheer a man to the echo, but the next day, when they find him friendly disposed toward Hindus, they [then] despise him.

6

Three Nations

(1)

A touch-me-not spirit pervades the atmosphere of this country; Nationalism cannot survive in this climate. A needle in the haystack can be found, but elements of nationalism cannot be traced in the Indian masses. It seems too that it is the common chain of slavery that binds them together; otherwise, there is no moral force to keep them united. One can well insinuate that Mr. Jinnah and I are of the same coin and do not wish well of this country and its people. Please yourself and think as you like, but truth is truth and must be told so that the realities may awaken the politicians to the danger facing this country. Our salvation does not lie in the theory of one nationhood or two. Why do we eulogize nationalism? It is as much a curse as communalism. Both nationalism and communalism dwarf the mind and make us bigots and blind. Last for dominance and sense of superiority are the offspring of nationalism. Nationhood goes before, and pride follows after it.

What is this untouchability and this caste system? This is pride lifted to the level of religious fanaticism. "My country, my community, my caste, right or wrong" are the products of a narrow civilization that is now leading [to bitterness] and strife. This modern departmentalism must end in smoke. But I do not want to make internationalism a cloak for inaction or a shield to be thrown over foreign dominations. Charity must begin at home, but it does not mean that I must conspire against a remote neighbor or try to cultivate a superiority complex in relation to the people who happen to be nearby. Nationalism has dragged the weak nations in the mire of humiliation. This exaggerated spirit of nationalism is responsible for untouchability in India. Nationalist Germany is astride a mountain of skulls and bones.

The more I ponder the treatment of the Sudras, the more I am convinced that, of all the sinners, the Hindu is the chief. The Musalman comes next. We Ahrars are not fighting for nationalism, but for internationalism. In us is awakened a conscience that feels a responsibility for the poverty and misfortune not of Indian people but of humanity as a whole. Communalism, Nationalism, and the caste system are the names of social and political diseases; they can only be remedied by sympathy. We have to do the duty that lies nearest to us. Hence, we are mainly devoted to the political emancipation of the Indian people. I don't think that Indians are one people, but still I feel called upon to serve Hindus and Muslims alike because they are my neighbors and living under the same political conditions. But for Sudras, I have great mercy and sympathy.

Don't try to convince me that Indian people are one nation. Nationalism is departmentalism; nevertheless, it denotes a wider group of people thinking alike and living like brothers. But in India, virulent individualism in fact rules the day. Everybody wishes to treat others as underdogs. There is no ordered system of ideas. There is no national pride but caste prejudices; still people have the audacity to say that Indians are one nation. Mere geographical conditions do not constitute a nation. There are three nations in India: the pure Hindus, the impure Sudras, and midway between the Muslims. A noble fear of seeming to be unpatriotic makes some hesitate to speak their whole mind on the subject. It is no doubt realized by all who have the capacity to (weigh) weight up facts and form a sound judgment of the present situation that there are not two but three nations in India — Hindus, Muslims, and Sudras. It is no good burking the fact that age-old prejudices cannot be shaken off in a few years.

The day of one nationhood may dawn on India, but we have no right to expect its dawn soon because we have not made any serious attempt to attain social unity. Social unity is a fact precedent to national harmony. Should we pray for a violent revolution that may destroy the social structure of India and bury the time-old prejudices forever? Here lies our salvation; otherwise, by evolutionary methods success cannot be achieved even within a reasonable period, and we will continue to be divided into three separate groups—Hindus, Musalmans, and Sudras. This prayed-for revolution must necessarily be based on economic justice; otherwise, the rich will continue to have the upper hand and turn the poor round their fingers as usual.

If social and economic reform is to progress at present at a snail's pace, then it must be noted that India's ills are not due to religion, but to the touch-me-not spirit of a great section of the Indian people. The present religion professed by the common Musalman is not the religion of the Prophet but is that religion that was evolved by Emperor Akbar in consultation with his Hindu advisors. In essence and spirit, it is Sanatan Dharma; the only difference seems to be that, in the case of Muslims, sentiment centers around the Prophet, and Hindus devote their prayers to Rama and Krishna. Some Hindu friends wrongly imagine that Musalmans are essentially a religious community and are influenced by religious people more than other communities. On the contrary, I see that religious people lead the Hindu masses. The Mahasabha section is led by Pandit Madan Mohan Malviaji, and the congressional section is led by Mahatma Gandhi; both of these gentlemen are essentially religious. There must be something wrong [with the] upper story [of anyone] who thinks that Mr. Jinnah is a religious man. So, religion has no hold on Muslims. They are bigoted against Hindus not because of religious motives but on account of social and economic boycotts by the Hindus that have laid them prostrate.

(2)

If the Indian people do not form one nation, they lose nothing; if they learn to live peacefully, they would gain everything. Different history, different social customs, even different languages should not mar our progress. I know that caste prejudices and untouchability are not be remedied soon, but their catastrophic results can be avoided. If Musalmans, instead of expecting every

Hindu to treat them as social equals, inculcate the spirit of responsive cooperation in their community, the situation will be eased within a few years. Instead of boycotting the Hindus as a community and treating them as impure and unclean, they should try to pay the arrogant Hindus in the same coin. Musalmans should not refuse to dine with those who do not treat them as untouchables. This will have a wholesome effect on the relations of both the communities. The number of those who believe in inter-dining will steadily increase, Muhammadans will have hope for the future, and their dignity will be saved for the present.

I know some of our Hindu brethren, instead of being ashamed of their treatment toward Musalmans, will dub them as bigots and communalists, but we must patiently endure it. These defensive tactics will not disturb the peace of the country. This must be clearly borne in mind that we are adopting a line of temporary politics in order to be immune from the evil effect of untouchability. For Sudras, I venture to prescribe the same medicine. But they are half-dead. We Hindus and Muslims have taken the life out of them. I have already advised them to take bold steps, but to whom is my advice directed? To Sudras, we have crushed their souls so much that they are now unable to hate and take revenge. By granting them separate electorates, the British Government wanted to resurrect them to serve their own purposes, but fate decided otherwise. Poor people will not be able to stand on their own feet for a long time to come without the aid of any friendly arm, and that aid will not come soon, I am sure.

Both Hindus and Muhammadans are still tough against them. Muhammadans, I am sorry to say, feel their own shoe when it pinches and do not feel the tight boot of the Sudras. Poverty is hard, but untouchability is horrible. We, along with Hindus, have made their lot hard and horrible. How keen and impatient the Muhammadans are to remove the taint of untouchability from themselves, but they are not half as earnest to remove this taint from the Sudras. If Muslims do not resent being bracketed with the Sudras, I would advise them to find common cause with them.

First, extend a helping hand toward the Sudras and embark on the scheme of responsible cooperation with Hindus so that we may be able to live in peace in this country. Unless the international spirit, in other words, the humanitarian spirit, pervades in the Hindu society, Muslim and Sudra must take a defensive line of action in order to be safe form the evil effects of untouchability. No doubt, all people of India have to sink and swim together politically, but Hindus have given free rein to their prejudices and claim not only a mental or moral superiority over others, but also consider others as unclean and impure.

A politician is a past master in the art of delay. Indian politicians are unwilling to take up the cause of those who are considered untouchables in earnest. A man of true feelings naturally fires up to see the treatment meted out to Musalmans by the Hindus and to the Sudras both by Hindus and Musalmans. Let not the silence of Musalmans and Sudras give consent to untouchability. The communities affected should leave no stone unturned to change their lot as soon as possible. All people are the architects of their own fortunes. We must frankly tell those who ill-treat others that the cup of patience has run over. Mend yourself, or we ourselves will end untouchability by resorting to responsive cooperation. This must be clearly borne in mind that social uplift cannot be derived only by the missionary work of the leaders of Congress; untouchables should also exert themselves to get out of this situation.

Unless all people in India attain equal social status, their political future will remain gloomy. It is a part of patriotism to resort to nonviolent noncooperation with those who think themselves highborn and look upon others as untouchables. No sooner do they come to their senses and relinquish their arrogance, it is our duty to lift the ban from them at once. Muhammadans are in a position to start this responsible cooperation with Hindus. They will become very strong in a few years' time, and they will never find reason to fight with Hindus as at present. Their present strife is absolutely social and economic and not religious or political. It is therefore right to remove the disease by starting responsive cooperation. That is to say, by continuing to dine with those who have no objection to dine with you, but refusing to take anything edible from the hands of those who consider you impure and unclean. All political struggles end in Hindu Muslim riots because Hindus and Muslims are not socially united. They will become friends in a short space of time provided Muhammadans act upon my advice or Hindus banish the idea of treating others as untouchables. Responsible cooperation is an easy affair, but it is expecting too much from the Hindus to give up [the] habit that has become their second nature.

Untouchability is a utilitarian superstition. This mold of thought is very valuable for those who practice it. It dries up the main artery of economic prosperity of those who are considered impure and unclean. The touchables will seldom buy anything from those who are considered untouchable. Hence, they condemn them to economic stagnation by refusing to trade with them. The prejudices of the high caste Hindus are very considered. They never question whether ghee is touched by Musalmans or Sudras. Milk, so long as it is not boiled, is pure to the Hindu even if a Sudra touches it. So, there is method in their madness. The ingenuity of the touchables was ever on the rack to keep others down without much inconvenience to themselves. By treating others as untouchables, the immaterial advantages of the Hindus increased with the passing of time; even Muhammadans were hard put to maintain equality with them.

Unless Muhammadans and Sudras devise some method to combat the evil ingenuity and the utilitarian prejudices of those Hindus, they will go to the dogs. Responsive cooperation is the only effective weapon to combat those who refuse to treat their countrymen as their equals. In a few years, Muhammadans have made marked progress in the field of politics, but they still require much to do in the field of economics. I cannot advise Muslims to cultivate the love for money in their minds. They should attempt to create a new world order based on economic justice. By bettering the lot of all the people in India, we can better our own lot. Muslim young men should at once join those bodies that aim at a better social order. If Muhammadans gird up their loins, being responsive [to] cooperation at once, and make up their minds to join hands with those who want to change the old economic order by peaceful methods, then and only then will peace reign in the country and this earth will become heaven for us all.

Hindus are not bad people. They are peace-loving and sympathetic. If once they are forced to give up the superstition of untouchability, they are sure to prove good neighbors. This certificate to Hindus will lash some of the Muslims to fury who think that the Hindu is incapable of giving up narrow ideologies, and they will say further that their interest cannot be safe in the keeping of those whose gains consist in the percentage of our losses and who have themselves held off all these years from cultivating our friendships. I am not a pessimist. I still believe that the old world order will yield place to a new. The social outlook of the Hindus will naturally be widened, but we must play our part to bring that day near. The popularity of the Pakistan scheme rests mainly on the treatment by Hindus; if once the Hindu is reformed, no one will hear of Pakistan in this country.

There are certain ulema who take exception to this Pakistan scheme because they think it would narrow their field of activity as missionaries. Muslims will hesitate to attach much value to it, because up to this time, their missionary zeal was zero. Not one percent of them treated their house sweepers as human beings, not to speak of delivering the message of Islam throughout the length and breadth of the country. Muhammadans openly declare that all of their woes are the dark fruit of untouchability practiced by Hindus and the unfair dealings of the cunning moneylenders who belong to the same class. They are ready to play even in the hands of imperialism if they are given hope to be saved from the man-made sufferings. British imperialism is not as bad as the humiliating treatment of our countrymen. Hindus may laugh scornfully at this unpatriotic idea. But untouchability is the very negation of patriotism.

Those of our countrymen who have no feelings, no emotion outside of their job of moneymaking, cannot appreciate the point of view of the poor Muslims. Those good-hearted Muslim theologians who put forward the plea of propagation of Islam against the Pakistan scheme seem to belong to the upper strata of society, and consequently fail to feel the pulse of the masses who suffer daily indignities at the hands of the Hindus. If the Muslim League is not merely shaking the tree in the hope of making some fine fruit fall and the Hindus continue the same treatment of Musalmans, Pakistan ought to be considered as an accomplished fact. Either the cowardice of the Muslim League leaders or a change of heart of the highborn Hindus can now alter the Pakistan situations.

There are some other well-meaning gentlemen in the Muslim Community who feel that the Pakistan scheme is financially unsound. To carry government with a deficit budget is an impossible affair. But if the top-heavy services are dispensed with and there is a will to work, no country in the world is such whose finances are insufficient to carry on the simple machinery of the government. If the conditions under which a community is made to live are suffocating, it is but natural that it will leave no stone unturned to find a breathing space without having regard to other inconveniences. Life is not worth living under humiliating conditions. Muhammadans will naturally choose to rule in the hell of Pakistan than to serve in the heaven of Hindustan.

Under the unitary system of government and with present social and economic order, Muhammadans will surely sink down soon to the depth of the Sudras. If the present social and economic order is to continue for a long time to come, then the Pakistan scheme will serve the purpose of Musalmans more than the unitary form of government. When discussing the scheme embodied in the Nehru Report, I, on behalf of those friends who now form the Ahrar group, made it clear in the General Meeting of the All Parties Conference held in Lucknow that the scheme of government embodied in the report would not serve the best interests of the country because it would raise grave doubts in the minds of the Musalmans as to their political future in this land. Musalmans did not attach any importance to my line of argument at that time, and Hindu politicians turned down my proposition based on federated provinces. A scheme of federation can only work well in a subcontinent like India. Provincial autonomy has now preceded the formation of representative government at the center. Muhammadans may now claim that less residuary powers be given to the center. The inauguration of the provincial autonomy has given a natural right to the provinces to break off at will from the rest of India. So, under the real federated scheme, Musalmans will practically live in a Pakistan. It will be up to Musalmans to decide whether they wish to live in Hindustan or to insist on a separate home for themselves.

To live in Pakistan or the Federated Hindustan will make no difference to the Muslims. If they propose to live in federated India, they live there for their own benefit. If their life is uncomfortable, they will naturally like to sever their connection with Hindu India. Hence, both from a national or communal point of view, the cry of Pakistan is ill-advised and ill-timed. We must get our liberty first and try for some time to honestly make up differences and affect a social and economic revolution. Every pound of our energy should be spent on making the Indian people a classless society. After swaraj, Muslims will not tolerate to live for a moment as untouchables. Social degradation is more pinching than slavery. After swaraj, which will be the natural outcome of this war, Muhammadans will become more desperate. Once politically free, they will resent this social treatment with double vigor and energy. Once a community becomes conscious of its humiliating treatment, it grows more and more vociferous with the passing of time. Every Hindu and nationalist Musalman should know that the Muslim community is becoming more conscious of the degrading social treatment day by day.

Though the Pakistan scheme is not without its dangers, but Muhammadans like to drift further away from their Hindu neighbors because they feel uncomfortable in the society of those who have not yet learned to treat their countrymen as their equals. The Federation of the autonomous provinces with less residuary powers at the center can best serve the purpose of Musalmans. It is certain that if the social treatment by the Hindus becomes what is desired, then the Musalman may be made to give more and more powers to the center. But if, on the advice of Hindu Maha Sabha, Hindus take into their heads to become more [unfair], in their dealings with Musalmans, then the Pakistan movement will gather strength.

Mr. Sirinawasa Iyenger, an ex-President of the Congress, is one of those well-meaning gentlemen who are still under the impression that the Hindu-Muslim problem is one of a political nature. Once the Musalmans are satisfied on the political issue, both the communities will learn to live amicably. He has gone so far as to suggest that Muhammadans be given half the share of the central government. I am one of those who humbly suggest that the Hindu-Muslim question is not one of a political nature, but rather one that has a social and economic basis. Economically serfs and socially humiliated, the Muslim community cannot be satisfied even if some people are raised to the most exalted positions. Even the masses will demand them to make laws for social leveling and economic justice at once. If present social and economic conditions are to continue, strife and struggle will go on unabated. Political rights without social and economic justice are meaningless. More shares in the center and more independence in the provinces must accompany a complete change of heart in the Hindu public. Otherwise, more political power to the

Muslims will bring them nearer to Hindus only to fight at close quarters.

There is always a cry that Islam is in danger. The man in the street who does not fully appreciate the teachings of religion feels himself called upon to make sacrifices for the sake of Islam. The East India Company, foreseeing the danger, proclaimed its intention of administering the personal law of the Muslims and Hindus through their own qazis and judges. It is necessary that it may be made known to the Muslim public that under the swaraj government they will have their own qazis to administer their personal law as in the time of the East India Company. On behalf of the Ahrar Party, their leaders invited the attention of other parties in the country to this demand. I know that the upper strata of the Muslims [are] not in favor of this demand because its members do not want their property to be administered in accordance with the law of Islam. It may be noted that Congress leaders are not against this demand, but the vocal section of the community is not enthusiastic about it, so nothing could be done in this respect after the Karachi Congress, which assured all communities to safeguard their personal laws.

In short, if Muslims get a proper share in the center, more power is given to the provinces, and personal laws of Muslims are administered through qazis, Muslims will be as secure in Hindustan as they would be in Pakistan, provided the governments in the provinces and centers are based on social and economic justice. Social tyranny and economic boycott ought to be considered cardinal sins in the country; otherwise, Muslim public opinion would continue to clamor for Pakistan, where they would hope to live in peace and freedom.

All the exponents of Pakistan contemplate letting the Hindus and Sikhs live side-by-side with them as at present. Hindus and Sikhs with present prejudices of untouchability will continue to make the Pakistan an Achutistan. Then, perhaps Musalmans will think of embarking on a new scheme of transfer of population. This cannot be done unless we endeavor to carry things with a high hand. Who can dare to think that the transfer of populations will be a smooth sailing? Is the present leadership of the Muslim League strong enough and willing to embody the spirit of sacrifice enough to force the issue?

The Muslim League always presented itself to me as a political club of idlers and parasites. They have not yet dreamed of the horrors that will follow the Pakistan scheme. They sit satiated with their heads full of castles in the air. They honestly hope that the British Government will make Pakistan a comfortable home for them. Gain without pain is the hope of those who live in a fool's paradise. Unless Muhammadans make up their minds to go through fire and water, their vainly imagined fancies will bear no fruit. But I offer a more practical proposition. A federated India with fewer powers at the center will result in a full dominion status for Musalmans. They can break off their connection at any time from Hindu India if they find that their lives have been made intolerable under the federal government. To contemplate the vivisection of India at this stage is urging the community to extreme measures without corresponding gain.

How long will we live a cat-and-dog life in India? I am glad to note that Mahatma Gandhi has wisely declared that the Pakistan scheme is no calamity. If we cannot live with each other like good neighbors, let us part as friends and live peaceful lives in our respective homes. To Muslims, I say, "Why should we put off the days of our salvation by discussing the utopian scheme of Pakistan, which has no practical value unless and until we throw off the foreign yoke?"

7

The Conclusion

T he old world order is dying. You will hear of it no more. Every cloud has a silver lining. War in Europe is sure to yield good results for humanity as a whole. We must look forward with hope. The world revolution will not revolutionize the mentality of the Indian people. Though we are weakened and eaten up from within, we may hope to emerge strong from this world conflict. We can recreate India, which may be a great asset for mankind. I am not halting between the two opinions and am frankly of the view that Hindus and Musalmans do constitute two separate nations at present; still, I hope that once we manage to rise from beneath the foreign heel, India may be able to lead the world to peace and prosperity.

There are some Muhammadans who feel that Hindus cannot be won over on any terms, and therefore they do not wish to try the chance. They think that vivisection of India is the only remedy. Through their social and economic boycotts, Musalmans are cast adrift upon the world without resources. Those Musalmans who speak in this strain should realize that government service has become the be-all and end-all of us all. We do not rely on our own energy and like Sycophants wish to bask in the sun of official favor. [A] Muslim was the soldier of God. He was the born leader of nations. But now the spirit of pleasure prevails over the spirit of sacrifice. They have forgotten that those who adhere at all costs to truth and sacrifice their all for the good of the people will soon find the promised land where all that they sacrificed is restored to them.

Why do Musalmans listen to the call of duty with the air of a man quite borne down with disappointment? It is Islam that teaches them never to be disappointed, and against all miseries, their spirit should bear up unbroken. I have frankly admitted the present atmosphere is quite suffocating for Muhammadans. It will require Herculean efforts to build a separate social and economic structure for the Muslim community in India, and I have suggested the remedy. The truth is that too great a faith has been placed by all political organizations in political advance and too little altogether in molding the present to ensure the future social harmony. The signs of the times are ominous. The intelligence of the Muslim must perceive the danger ahead. A happy, quiet life after their own hearts is possible only after struggle. You have to pull a nation to its feet that has been centuries deep in rot, and that ought to be done courageously and cautiously.

With the unmistakable certainty of a dreamer, we have to carry out our scheme of social and economic revolution, but we must not declare war on Hindu society. We have every right to cure our society of Hindu-made sufferings, but at the same time, we must take care not to create bad blood between the communities. Hindus are ostentatiously wrong in treating the Musalman as untouchable, but we should not behave like a man beside himself. We have to convince the Hindu that we are not satisfied with this treatment, and at the same time, we have to give proof of our good intentions by our benevolent deeds.

We must live the lives of true Muslims who are the friends of all and enemies of none, ever ready to offer a helping hand to all who are needy. Social services to all alike should be our proud badge of distinction. We still have to do a great deal to banish fear and doubt from the hearts of our Hindu neighbors who are always suspicious of our political designs. Tell them frankly that the Pakistan scheme is gaining impetus because of their treatment of the Musalmans, but never hesitate to serve your Hindu countrymen. You must know in your heart of hearts that the Pakistan scheme is the outcome of the defeatist mentality and can be our last resort if we fail to change the hearts of Hindus.

Otherwise, the best course for us is to become leaders of the Indian people not by the dint of brute force, but through service and sacrifice. Show your Islamic character by treating all people kindly. Refuse to be treated as an untouchable, but at the same time make up your mind to treat Sudras as human beings. Lip sympathy and mere generosity of outlook will not do any good for the Sudras. We must lay low the demon of untouchability and set them free from its clutches. Obliterate all prejudices of the past. Know that God is angry with us because we are also responsible for the present inhuman treatment of human beings. Let us go down on our knees, ask pardon of the Sudras for our past conduct, and beg Almighty God to help us in treating the lowly-born people as equal partners in a new social order. For the ill-treatment of our countrymen, we have been punished with foreign domination. We must turn over a new leaf, mend our ways, and learn to live with our neighbors, especially the Sudras, as brothers. Then and then alone, a new era will dawn upon us. We have lost Hindustan; we will lose even Pakistan if we do not say good-bye to our slave mentality and become the true soldiers of Islam.

Brothers in faith! The majority of the Musalmans live in Pakistan already. We have our majority provinces. We are nine scores in number but have no resolution to live the life of true Musalmans. We should abhor cherishing the idea of subjugating nations, but we must try to maintain our superiority over others through high morals, great sacrifices, and continued service. We are not to exploit others, but to win over the hearts of the communities by kind treatment. Aspire only to become leaders of the people. Never covet to lay hands on the crowns of kings or greedily look to the wealth of the nations. Distribute the wealth equally, and treat Muslims and non-Muslims justly.

We have to lead the world to prosperity and peace; therefore, we must make our character sublime. We have to drag out humanity from the mire of misery. Let us try to live in India as a community that is morally strong and ready to render every help to those who stand in need of it. To live a helpless life and to be treated as untouchables is shameful for a Musalman. We must first blot out untouchability and win the freedom of India, and after that, if we see that Hindu society is still tough and means to continue the same treatment of us as before, we have every right to partition India into two comfortable homes—Hindustan and Pakistan.

But where is that promised land? What are its boundaries? No one knows and perhaps will not know until doomsday. We must not run after mirages but try to live in India as good citizens and morally strong people. We must join hands with the lower strata of the other communities and clamor for social leveling and economic justice. I am sure that the Nawabs and Knights of my own community will turn down any advice because they themselves do not believe in social leveling and economic justice. Hindu capitalists want a Hindustan where they may be able to safely lord over the destinies of the poorer classes of all the communities. Musalmans of high houses likewise want a Pakistan where they may exploit and rule the lower classes of the Hindus and the Musalmans alike. Sikhs of the upper classes also want a Punjab where they may comfortably rule and exploit Hindu, Muslim, and Sikh masses.

The partition of India is, in fact, the cry of the upper classes of all three communities. It is not a communal demand as some people think, but a stunt in order that the poorer classes may not concentrate their thoughts and energies on all-important questions of social and economic justice. It will be a very sad day for the masses of this country when the League and the Congress will cease the glove fight and the capitalists of both the communities join hands to exploit the people. This fight of the upper classes is a blessing in disguise. May God perpetuate it for the good of the masses.

But we Ahrars must not lose time in merely taking stock of the situation and go on criticizing what the great guns of Congress and the big drums of the League say and do. We represent those whose lips are sealed by the cares of tomorrow and for whom this world has become the vale of tears. Therefore, it is our duty to boldly come forward and declare to the world that Ahrars stand for the following programs:

(1) equal distribution of the wealth of the country;
(2) removal of untouchability; and
(3) respect for every religion and complete autonomy to live according to Shariat.

If the Hindu community in any way thwarts our way, then and only then should we join hands with Mr. Jinnah and raise the slogan of Pakistan. Muslims now refuse to live as economic serfs of the Hindus, and as their social untouchables. Though we know that Pakistan is an impracticable scheme, we will make up our differences with the Muslim League and fight those forces that keep us down. We are fighting for the freedom of India, and at the same time, we declare that Muhammadans will not live as underdogs of any community or class.

THE END

Chaudhry Afzal Haq, May 1941
Mufakkir-e-Ahrar
Humanitarian and "Thinker" of the Ahrar Party

Flag of the British Raj flying over India on January 8, 1942, the day of Chaudhry Afzal Haq's funeral in Lahore, Punjab, British India.

Source: Courtesy of Wikipedia

Message from Chaudhry Afzal Haq.

"Pakistan is the voice of anguished hearts, and you must not oppose it."

Chaudhry Afzal Haq

"We must live the lives of true Muslims who are the friends of all and enemies of none, ever ready to offer a helping hand to all who are needy."

Chaudhry Afzal Haq
Pakistan and Untouchability

A message of tolerance for the diversity of the human family

The National flags that follow represent the New Nations born from the struggle and sacrifices given by so many, to achieve so much, with a newly freed Indian subcontinent after 1947.

May these new nations of the subcontinent never forget the sacrifices made for all of us and may we remember to honor our religious and ethnic diversity by teaching our children to live cooperatively with each other in peace and social harmony.

National flag of Pakistan
Source: Courtesy of Wikipedia

National flag of India
Source: Courtesy of Wikipedia

National flag of Bangladesh
(Formerly East Pakistan)

Source: Courtesy of Wikipedia

National Flag of Myanmar
(Formerly Burma)
Source: Courtesy of Wikipedia

Dedication

With the republishing of Pakistan and Untouchability, we honor the monumental sacrifices made by all the men, women and their families who gave their lives and their futures for the freedom of the people of the Indian sub-continent, regardless of religion or ethnic origin.

Let us build on this honorable legacy of sacrifice and selflessness together.

Producers & Editors notes

Forgive me in advance for any errors I have made or edits I have missed. I humbly submit to you that I am no literary scholar and have done this work with love in my heart and in honor and memory of my dear grandfather, Chaudhry Afzal Haq.

Arif (Art) Khan, Producer & Editor, Pakistan and Untouchablity (2014 International version).

Notes:

1) Chaudhry Afzal Haq is pronounced as: *Chaudh-ree Auf-zul Huck.*
2) Our goal was to edit as little content as possible in order to keep the original style and feel of the book for the reader of today. The edits made were done to improve readability of the book for a new Facebook generation. Considering the first edition of this book was rushed into publication in 1941 and at a time just before our grandfathers passing, his writing style impressed me. It is his last book written at the end of a life, by an author who wrote 15 other books in Urdu only. This was the only English book he had ever published.
3) All edits are outlined in [brackets] to ensure todays reader can appreciate how little editing was actually needed.
4) The dates of historical events that were used in the introduction were the best dates we could determine based on various interviews done over the past 3 years.
5) Note: Many supposed "Untouchables" converted as Christians and in this case, Christians and Muslims were faced with the same discrimination in British India.
6) *Reference for quotes in the introduction of this book are from Abu Yousaf Qasmi, Chaudhry Afzal Haq

Editors acknowledgement

Thank you goes to Michael Bahr who was a good friend to the project and an editorial advisor during the republishing of this book.

www.ingramcontent.com/pod-product-compliance
Lightning Source LLC
Chambersburg PA
CBHW060413290526
45791CB00002B/738